Contents

P9-DHL-439

FROM DIGITAL NATIVES TO
DIGITAL WISDOM

Hopeful Essays for
21st Century Learning

MARC PRENSKY

Foreword by MILTON CHEN

CORWIN
A SAGE Company

CORWIN
A SAGE Company

FOR INFORMATION:

Corwin
A SAGE Company
2455 Teller Road
Thousand Oaks, California 91320
(800) 233-9936
Fax: (800) 417-2466
www.corwin.com

SAGE Ltd.
1 Oliver's Yard
55 City Road
London EC1Y 1SP
United Kingdom

SAGE India Pvt. Ltd.
B 1/I 1 Mohan Cooperative
Industrial Area
Mathura Road, New Delhi
India 110 044

SAGE Asia-Pacific Pte. Ltd.
33 Pekin Street #02-01
Far East Square
Singapore 048763

Acquisitions Editor: Debra Stollenwerk
Associate Editor: Desirée A. Bartlett
Editorial Assistant: Kimberly Greenberg
Production Editor: Cassandra Margaret Seibel
Copy Editor: Pam Suwinsky
Typesetter: C&M Digitals (P) Ltd.
Proofreader: Barbara Johnson
Indexer: Gloria Tierney
Cover Designer: Scott Van Atta
Permissions Editor: Adele Hutchinson

Copyright © 2012 by Marc Prensky

All rights reserved. When forms and sample documents are included, their use is authorized only by educators, local school sites, and/or noncommercial or nonprofit entities that have purchased the book. Except for that usage, no part of this book may be reproduced or utilized in any form or by any means, electronic or mechanical, including photocopying, recording, or by any information storage and retrieval system, without permission in writing from the publisher.

Author photo on page ix by Robert Leslie.

Printed in the United States of America.

Library of Congress Cataloging-in-Publication Data

Prensky, Marc.

From digital natives to digital wisdom : hopeful essays for 21st century learning / Marc Prensky ; foreword by Milton Chen.

p. cm.

Includes bibliographical references and index.

ISBN 978-1-4522-3009-2 (pbk.)

1. Educational change—United States. 2. Education—Aims and objectives—United States. 3. Education—Effect of technological innovations on—United States. I. Title.

LA217.2.P68 2012
370.973—dc23   2011048360

This book is printed on acid-free paper.

Certified Chain of Custody
SUSTAINABLE FORESTRY INITIATIVE
Promoting Sustainable Forestry
www.sfiprogram.org
SFI-01268

SFI label applies to text stock

12 13 14 15 16 10 9 8 7 6 5 4 3 2 1

Foreword

It's a wonderful honor to write the Foreword for Marc Prensky's new book, *From Digital Natives to Digital Wisdom: Hopeful Essays on 21st Century Learning.* Marc is a provocative and prolific writer, marvelous speaker, and a courageous digital child advocate. He has the same passionate energy and courage of conviction as other child advocates I've known, such as Marian Wright Edelman of the Children's Defense Fund and Fred Rogers in public TV. He shares their same DNA and righteous indignation at the injustices that adults perpetrate on children. Marc continually tells us to take off our pretentious adult glasses, get down to the children's level, and see these curious, playful beings as the marvelous learning machines they are. If he started an organization, it might well be called the Digital Natives Defense Fund.

This book collects Marc's own digital wisdom from essays written over the years. It ought to be packaged with every new computer and smartphone sold to educators, just like they used to put a sample of Tide detergent in new washing machines. Like that little box of soap, this book is the active ingredient that can help educators use their new devices more effectively.

When starting up our *Edutopia* magazine in 2005, we turned to Marc as one of the most insightful writers we knew. Several of his essays, such as "Simulation Nation" and "The True 21st Century Literacy Is Programming," first appeared in the magazine and on the Edutopia.org website and always attracted lively commentary from readers.

It's revealing to me to reread these essays and see the scope and evolution of Marc's thinking. In practicing what he preaches, Marc has been open to new ideas and trends and to adjusting his thinking based on new information. The past decade has certainly brought a rush of new digital platforms and tools, from YouTube to Facebook and Twitter. And with the global shift of power, it's abundantly clear that we need to prepare children for life and work in a world we can't predict. (I myself sometimes tire of the continuing parade of platforms and would like to create my own, simplifying their best features for digital immigrants, and call it YouTwitFace.)

It's hard to believe that Marc's essay "Digital Natives, Digital Immigrants" was published 10 years ago and that a new generation of Digital Natives is entering our schools. The need for the educational system and those working in it to see its learners differently has become even more urgent. The fissures in the system are widening, and the days of the conventional classroom are clearly numbered. I particularly love his metaphor that the system needs a Delete button (a big one, in fact). Like so many Prenskyisms, it's an unforgettable way of encapsulating a key issue. We keep adding more programs, initiatives, and technologies, but we rarely eliminate the outdated policies and practices that prevent us from embracing the future.

Another gem is "Turning On the Lights," in which he gives voice to the fundamental problem so many students have with school: sheer boredom. He describes the rapidly growing divide between the knowledge kids can attain out of school and the narrow confines of their lives within it. And in "Simulation Nation," he poses part of the solution: to embed learning in the types of game-based experiences that students flock to on their own. Whether we will invest in creating these new online worlds in which students can explore and collaborate indeed represents a key to the future of our nation.

In the Epilogue, perhaps the most provocative essay, "From Digital Natives to Digital Wisdom," Prensky stretches his own digital muscles and peers into the future. Can the new generation of digital tools extend our senses and enhance our capacities, and, in essence, make us better, more compassionate people? I share Marc's hopeful vision for this future and believe that with pathfinders like him, we have a better chance of creating that wiser, more peaceful world.

Milton Chen
Senior Fellow,
The George Lucas Educational
Foundation and Chairman,
Panasonic Foundation

About the Author

Marc Prensky is an internationally acclaimed speaker, writer, consultant, visionary, and innovator in the field of education and learning. Marc's professional focus is on reinventing the learning process, designing new pedagogy and curriculum for the digital generation, and combining the motivation of new technology, video games, and other highly engaging activities with educational and business content. Considered one of the world's leading experts on the connection between technology and learning, Prensky was called by *Strategy+Business* magazine "that rare visionary who implements."

Prensky looks at education from the perspective of the receivers (that is, the students) rather than just the providers. He focuses on how to teach and motivate today's students, and on how to motivate and reinvigorate their teachers as well. Prensky promotes a new form of partnership between teachers and students, and, through his writings and talks, helps teachers learn to change their pedagogy to ways that are far more effective for 21st century students.

Marc also focuses on how to teach future-oriented skills—including problem solving, partnering, collaborating in online communities, video making, and programming—as an integrated part of all curricula. He is a strong partisan of teachers' knowing and using students' individual passions as motivators and of students' participation in the design of their own education.

In his talks around the globe, Marc initiates and conducts unique educator–student dialogues about the teaching and learning process. His innovative combination of pedagogy and technology—including game technology, where he was an early pioneer—is becoming increasingly accepted and used by educators worldwide as the wave of the future.

Marc's background includes master's degrees from Yale University, Middlebury College, and the Harvard Business School *with distinction*. He has taught at all levels, from elementary to college, and ran a prototype charter school in East Harlem, New York.

Marc also performed on Broadway and at Lincoln Center, worked on Wall Street, and spent six years as a corporate strategist and product development director with the prestigious Boston Consulting Group. After all that, he is thrilled to be back working in the field of education and learning.

Marc is a native New Yorker, where he lives with his wife Rie, a Japanese writer, and their son Sky, a thriving student New York City's public schools.

To Rie, for inspiring all these thoughts

Introduction

I have a vision for education (and, of course, so do lots of folks ☺). But my vision differs from most people's in one very significant respect: My vision is bottom-up—it begins with the students—what *they* need and how we can give it to *them*. I want our young people to succeed in *their* 21st century, which will be, without a doubt, a turbulent one, characterized by variability, uncertainty, chaos, and ambiguity (what my good friend, former school superintendent David Engle, calls "VUCA") and by increasingly accelerating change.

Adapting to this new context of change, variability, and uncertainty is the biggest challenge we are now facing—as educators and as people. It is something that almost none of us is used to—unless, of course, we were born in the 21st century. So I try hard, in my thinking and writing, to see education through the eyes of those who *were* born in this century (or almost)—through the eyes, that is, of the students who are receiving our education rather than through the eyes of their elders who provide it. I have come to see clearly that the conclusions about education one draws from this alternative perspective are very different from the ones nearly all educators, politicians, and parents are currently drawing.

Listening to Our Students

The most important thing I have learned from carefully re-observing education in my later years is how little most educators *really listen* to the kids they teach (although a great many of those educators think they do). As part of my talks I conduct "student panels," in which a group of local students answers questions onstage as their educators first listen and then ask questions of their own—I have now done scores of these. Sadly, in most cases it is the *first time* that the students and educators in that district, system, state, or even country have *ever* had an student–educator dialogue about how they teach and how their kids want to learn (as opposed to about specific details and grades).

I believe strongly that if we did listen to our students' opinions on this, and did have such dialogues universally—and, more importantly, if we acted on what we heard—we would do things very differently. Not that our young people have all the answers—they don't. But they do have the educational needs. We adults have educational needs, too, but a very different set. Adults have needs such as being able to demonstrate "educational effectiveness" (that is, that we are "getting the kids up to grade") and "keeping our country competitive." (Actually, many of what adults call "educational needs" are far more about the adults than about the kids.) The kids just need and want the skills and tools to succeed in their own times and lives.

To the disappointment of some (and the delight of many), the vision I have is not just about technology in education. In fact, it is not even just a vision of better education. My vision is one of *better people*, better equipped to face the challenges of the world they will live in—that is, a world far different than yesterday's or even today's. Technology has an important place in that vision, because it has an important place in our future. But it does not dominate the vision; rather it supports it. As one of my student panelists put it brilliantly: "We see technology as a foundation. It underlies everything we do." In the end, I am far more interested in creating important, useful learning and life opportunities for our students than I am in promoting *any* educational technology. (Except, of course, when technology helps achieve those things.)

Inspiring Teachers

A key element of realizing and implementing my vision has become—increasingly—inspiring and motivating teachers. Although I believe that *all* adults should play a role in educating our youth, the greatest hope for the 55 million kids in America (and the billion+ kids in the world) lies with the people with whom they spend a great many of their most formative years. What our teachers offer our students—that is, how teachers view their students and how they see their mission with them—will have an enormous influence on the world to come. Despite what some critics may wish for, we are not going to suddenly recruit and retain a "better" group of teachers—we have, in the main, a group of highly dedicated people who have chosen education as their life's work. My goal is not to waste or destroy this precious resource but to support it and make the most of it.

Most of our teachers require neither punishment nor replacement, but what they do need is new perspectives and ideas that work. Our educational context has changed, and a new context demands new thinking. This is what I try to provide.

It is critical, though, to understand that because the locus of "knowledge" has, in the 21st century, moved to a great extent from the teacher to the Internet, and because the personal passions of our 21st century students have become the kids' best (and often their only) motivation to learn, our teachers' job—in fact their very *raison d'être*—is going through enormous change. Rather than trying to insert knowledge into our kids' heads, as in the past (and then to measure how much of it got there), today's teachers need to find ways to create 21st century citizens (and workers) who parrot less and think more. This requires fully integrating into our teaching "meta" skills like critical thinking, problem solving, video, and programming, just as we now integrate reading and writing. To make this happen, teachers and students will need to work together in new forms of "partnering" in which students do what they do best—for example, use technology, find information, and create products that demonstrate their understanding—and in which teachers guide students by doing what they do best—for example, asking the right questions, putting things into the proper context, and ensuring quality and rigor.

Moving their practice into the new context for education can be—and is—exhilarating for most teachers. But it is also challenging.

Some protest that they are prevented from doing what they want to do, and know they should do, by the current atmosphere of proscribed curriculum and testing. I agree that this atmosphere is not helpful. Yet I believe strongly that there are ways to accommodate those requirements and still teach in a way that motivates our students to prepare themselves for the future. In fact, our success at doing this will be the strongest argument for removing those unhelpful barriers.

I truly believe that when most teachers understand that *the new context* is the cause of our educational problems—and that that is why many of their old practices no longer work as expected—they will figure out what to do differently. This is particularly true, I have seen, if they are offered good examples and suggestions. What our teachers need is the freedom to implement what they know to be right.

Certainly, the results of teaching in a modern way that connects with 21st century students can excite and stimulate educators. I receive many emails from teachers who have come away from my talks and writings newly energized and exhilarated. Many now say, as one teacher nicely put it, that "I used to teach my subject. Now I teach my students." Several have expressed that my ideas, particularly around connecting more deeply with students, have brought them back to the reasons they went into teaching in the first place. I am thrilled to find this happening.

I firmly believe that the new teaching roles that the 21st century offers are *so* much better, *so* much more powerful, and *so* much more interesting than what came before, that most teachers will, once they get their heads around those roles, rush to embrace them.

Not Easy

But getting one's head around new roles and approaches is not always easy. Change is difficult for all of us, particularly those not used to it. As psychologist Ron Evans points out, change involves not only learning new perspectives and behaviors but also grieving and mourning for those things we liked, found valuable, and were good at that no longer work (lecturing, for example). I believe, in fact, that what teachers need to do is best described not as "changing," but rather as "adapting" to the new context and environment we all find ourselves in. And I believe that to adapt most quickly and easily, teachers must search continually for the types of "easy-to-do/high-impact" steps I describe in the essay "Simple Changes in Current Practices May Save Our Schools."

Yet even as teachers *become* motivated to adapt and move forward, it is not always obvious how to change old habits. So this is an area where I try to provide help as well. For example, I have found that some of our best models of how to teach already exist in many of our classrooms. Good elementary teachers, good music and art teachers (and our best teachers in general) rarely lecture; they almost always let their students create "by and for themselves" with the teacher's guidance. We need to study and follow their prescient example.

All 21st century teachers must deal with the difficult issue that much of what educators thought was important in the past—and therefore put in place as things for young people to learn—has changed, and, in many cases, lost its value. Our kids certainly feel this, and so do more and more of today's instructors.

So as I progress and learn, I search for more and better ways to give teachers guidance—goals to reach for and paths to follow to reach them. My strong belief is that once teachers *understand* the new goals for our students, many—hopefully most—will, as they should, invent their own paths to reach them. "Just tell me where you want me to go, and let me get there in my own way" is something that I hear frequently not just from students but from teachers as well. Just as with students, some teachers require more help ("scaffolding" in schoolese) than others until they can do it on their own, so I try to offer this as well.

My main tool for encouraging adaptation is my writing. So I am extremely pleased to find this book in your hands and your mind open, I hope, to the ideas it contains.

In these essays I write about what I think needs to be done to improve our kids' education. I try to say this in as straightforward and jargon-free way as possible, so that everyone—teachers, parents, politicians, and others—can understand my meaning, and, I hope, be inspired to make positive changes based on my ideas. I search for memorable words and phrases that will help motivate readers to put an end to our old education that no longer works, replacing it with something far, far better.

At the very center of this shift stand our teachers. This is because the true changes we need will not come from tweaking or changing "the system" (although in some cases that may help). The real changes our kids require will only come, in America and the world, *from what every teacher does differently in every classroom.*

Thinking Long Term

This book unites many of the ideas I consider my most important. It includes my thoughts on the changing context of education and on what that implies about changing *how* we teach, and *what* we teach. My essays are intended to help people—not just teachers, *all* people— see education from a different perspective—I hope a more useful perspective—and, from that new perspective, to arrive on their own at new insights and ideas about what to do differently.

Whenever possible, I try to write (and think) about education for the long term. Although it is important, and often useful, to talk about what is currently going on, I realize that some of the things I talk about—specific technologies and products, for example—will soon be superseded (if they haven't been already), and that some of the seemingly urgent educational conflicts of the moment will go away. I try, therefore, as much as possible, to put forth educational ideas that I hope will last. I am honored that the terms "Digital Natives" and "Digital Immigrants" are still capturing people's attention—drawing both praise and criticism—more than a decade after I coined them ("Digital Natives, Digital Immigrants: Parts I and II"). In what I consider a huge compliment, someone recently emailed me that my piece about learning ("On Learning") "held up well" after nine years—an eternity in these times of change.

Some General Observations

As I have traveled and talked with hundreds of students and educators, certain "big" ideas have come into more and more focus for me and have taken a larger place in my writing. For example:

- Talking with students in the United States and around the world exposed me to how little students' opinions are listened to and taken into account. So I often now write in their defense (for example, "To Educate, We Must Listen").
- Closely observing young peoples' game playing and other habits convinced me that what is taking place in education is not a "dumbing down" of this generation but rather a huge, continuous change to new and different things becoming important. I often publicly debate this with Mark Bauerlein, the author of *The Dumbest Generation* (a title, and term, that I find particularly disrespectful).
- Looking closely at how today's students learn led me to the unexpected observation that the very process of learning—the crux of what we are all about as educators—is still very poorly understood. I found that what people think we "know" about learning is based on a huge variety of often conflicting theories, many of which apply more to groups (i.e., to classrooms) than to individual students. So I continue to search for more understanding in this area ("On Learning").
- Observing what goes on in our classrooms and hearing kids talk about their experiences led me to the conclusion that there are huge problems with *how* we teach, which is still, primarily, through an outdated "lecture" or "telling" style very much at odds with how today's students learn. This led me to the

concept of "partnering," which is the core of my book *Teaching Digital Natives: Partnering for Real Learning.*

- Reflecting on technology's role in education led me—despite my being a strong proponent of using digital technology for learning—to the distressing conclusion that our educators, in their push to get our classrooms and education up to date, too often add technology before the teachers know, pedagogically, what to do with it. Unfortunately, because of the speed with which our technology now moves, this often leads to the technology's becoming obsolete before it can ever add value. So despite huge financial investments, educational technology is often not realizing its great promise to improve our kids' education. I therefore think about the role technology *should* play in the learning process; my answer: technology only helps when it supports a pedagogy of "partnering" ("The Role of Technology in Teaching and the Classroom").

- Above all, thinking about what students need to know and do in the 21st century has shown me clearly that the deepest underlying problem with our current education is neither how we teach, nor the still-missing technology—rather it's *what* we teach. Our educators and students are stuck—for many historical reasons—with a curriculum that is highly outdated and of very little use in preparing our kids for the lives they will be facing. The Herculean struggle to get our kids to learn this mostly "useless" stuff, and to get "up to grade in it," is taking up, and wasting, almost all our time and effort. As a result, much of what today is touted as "educational reform" is really just "rearranging the deck chairs on the Titanic": we are applying Band-Aids to an education that is in need of a blood transfusion. Even the many well-intentioned proposals to add on "21st century skills" are not truly helpful, since without first deleting we have no room to add anything ("The Reformers Are Leaving Our Schools in the 20th Century").

Have My Ideas Changed?

A question I continually asked myself when rereading each of these essays for the book is, "Have my ideas changed since I wrote this?" I found that, in most cases, they haven't—I still believe strongly what I wrote. But occasionally they have, and I find this good, because *some* ideas, like *some* parts of education, *should* evolve with the changing times and context. In the cases where my thinking has evolved, I have commented on this in that essay's introduction. I have also, in a few places, gone back and done some minor rewriting in order to clarify points and to make the language more consistent with my current writing and thinking. This is indicated as well. But most of the essays stand as originally written.

Organization of the Book

The essays in the book are organized into two parts. The first, titled "Rethinking Education," contains some of my more "philosophical" writings about what education is, what needs to change in the 21st century to improve it, and why. Although it is easy—and even fashionable—to argue that schools should disappear, I take the position that for many practical reasons they won't, and so we had better improve them. In the second part, entitled "21st Century Learning, and Technology in the Classroom," I get to more specific issues about what I think can, and should, be done, for the benefit—always—not of the test scores but of the kids.

The book starts with "The Reformers Are Leaving Our Schools in the 20th Century," an essay that I felt compelled to write as I watched more and more well-meaning people who want to "reform" education—from presidents, to secretaries of education, to many politicians and philanthropists—go down the wrong educational path, wasting huge resources in the process. Next comes "On Learning," an earlier essay that makes the point of how little we in fact know about what we educators "think" we do. (Surprisingly, this is true *not* just at the neuroscience level, where we are still near the beginning of our understanding, but, far more importantly, at the behavioral level, where educators *can* work and modify their practices.) The essay that follows, "Education as Rocket Science," offers a new, much more positive way to look at our students (and teachers) than the negatives we far too often hear. I discuss what is needed to get these "rockets" to take off and fly far in the essay "Turning On the Lights."

Next, in the now "classic" essays "Digital Natives, Digital Immigrants: Parts I and II," I present the idea that students have changed and discuss why. I then further develop the "story" of these Digital Natives in "The Emerging Online Life of the Digital Native," and in "Young Minds, Fast Times." I point to some challenges for educators in "Blame Our Young? Or Use Their Passion!" and in "To Educate, We Must Listen." Part 1 concludes with two further challenges, first to curriculum designers ("Bringing the Future to School: The Prensky Challenge"), and then to today's educational philanthropists, who, I am very afraid, are wasting one of our greatest educational bounties and opportunities of all time ("Open Letter to the Bill & Melinda Gates Foundation").

In the book's second, more "practical" part, I begin with the important question, What is "The Role of Technology in Teaching and the Classroom" in the 21st century? I emphasize that while technology is crucial for our kids' future, the understanding that too many educators have of its role is problematic. In a similar vein, the essay "Backup Education?" counters the oft-heard opinion from educators that we should continue teaching all the "old stuff" for those relatively rare occasions when technology breaks down. The next essay, "Simple Changes in Current Practices May Save Our Schools," offers the powerful idea that there are a number of small changes that every teacher can make that will have an enormous impact on our kids' education.

The final essays in Part 2 deal with changes in our educational environment and context that don't receive, in my view, the level of attention and understanding they deserve. The first of these is the arrival of "short video" as a new two-way communication form ("Why YouTube Matters"). The second is the importance of computer and video games in our students' lives. Here I emphasize both the value the games bring to kids' learning and education ("Beyond the Lemonade Stand") and the problems kids often encounter when trying to get that learning acknowledged by their parents and educators ("On Being Disrespected"). I also offer a chart of "Types of Learning and Possible Game Styles" to aid in the design of better educational games.

In "Let's Be 'Digital Multipliers,'" I address the concern of many teachers about the so-called digital divide. In "Search Versus Research," I address teachers' fears about their students' unthoughtful use of the Internet. I conclude Part 2 with discussions of three additional technologies that I believe will shape our kids' 21st century education for the better: simulation ("Simulation Nation"), mobile devices ("What Can You Learn From a Cell Phone? Almost Anything!"), and programming ("The True 21st Century Literacy Is Programming").

The book's Epilogue, "From Digital Natives to Digital Wisdom: *Homo Sapiens Digital*," presents a hopeful view of the quickly coming era when all students and educators will be born in the 21st century—and will therefore, by definition, be "Digital Natives." I suggest in that essay that the question we should ponder for that future is no longer *whether* to use the technologies of our time but rather *how* to use them to become better, wiser people.

Included at the end of each part are a dozen questions intended to encourage you to reflect on the material you have just read and to look for your own solutions. These questions should also prove helpful to any individual or group using the book in "study" mode.

 প্ল প্ল ৪০ ৪০

While many today seek changes in our education, a huge question, mostly left unasked, is "What in education should evolve and change with the times, and what should not?" As we quest for a better, 21st century education for today's and tomorrow's children, figuring out the best solution to this thorny problem is perhaps our biggest educational challenge. In my view, most of today's education reformers, when they bother asking this question at all, get it wrong. In order for us to get it right we will need a lot more of what we typically call "wisdom"—perhaps even "digital wisdom." My hope is that—at least in some ways—you will find elements of this wisdom, both digital and otherwise, in these essays.

If you do, I hope you will take action based on what you learn. But if you don't, and you disagree, I'd like to hear from you as to where and why, because getting to a 21st century education requires not only new ideas but also dialogue and discussion—and, when we reach consensus, collaboration. Many smart people I know despair of ever getting public education to the place we require and are looking for different ways to prepare our kids for the future. But I remain an optimist. I believe that we *can* move education—both public and private—ahead to something far better, even though, as we all know, there are many obstacles to overcome in order to make that happen.

Although some advocate just dumping all our schools and doing education completely differently, the insurmountable barrier to doing this, at least for now, is that we need to keep our kids safe while we—their parents—work. That is why, even with the introduction of more and more advanced technology, school is unlikely to soon disappear. (Eventually, I believe, we will figure out ways to accomplish this, and then all bets are off.)

But if school remains a requirement in our and our kids' lifetimes, and we *don't* change what goes on in each of our classrooms, we abandon America's 55 million kids, and their kids, and kids throughout the world, to the education of the past. This I am unwilling to do.

I have great faith in our young people. I see a great new educational day coming, *from* them, *for* them, and *with* them. If my ideas hasten that day in any way, I will be happy.

So welcome to this collection of my thoughts and ideas. I hope you enjoy reading them, and please always feel free to send me your feedback at marcprensky@gmail.com.

PART 1

Rethinking Education

1

The Reformers Are Leaving Our Schools in the 20th Century

Why most U.S. school reformers are on the wrong track, and how to get our kids' education right for the future

Published in SNS Newsletter

I was compelled to write this opening essay after watching our leaders, again and again, offer solutions to our educational problems that left our education, and our children, mired in the past. My previous experience as a business strategy consultant helped me see, as I had for other industries, just how little of what we currently do—that is, of the education we provide to our children—helps us reach our goals and meet our future needs. I view our biggest educational need not as raising test scores, but as preparing our children for the future (although often conflated, those goals are not the same). Moreover, unfortunately, in today's world, those goals are increasingly at odds. This essay provides my overview of this dysfunctional situation and its causes, and offers, in a big-picture view, my solutions for fixing it. (Note: *I have made one significant change to the original published version: my original "3 C's" are now the "3 P's." I made this change when I found that someone else had already proposed a different 3 C's.*)

෬ ෬ ෨ ෨

What President Obama said:
"We need to out-educate."

What Obama should have said:
"We can't win the future with the education of the past."

This is an unprecedented time in U.S. education, and awareness that we have a problem has never been higher. Billions of dollars of public and private money are lined up for solutions. But I am convinced that, with our present course, when all that momentum and money is spent, we shall nonetheless end up with an educational system that is incapable of preparing the bulk of our students for the issues and realities they will face in the 21st century.

The reason is that the educational improvement efforts now in place are aimed at bringing back the education that America offered students in the 20th century (with some technological enhancements). Sadly, too many people assume this is still the "right" education for today, although it no longer works for most of our students. Despite the many educational projects and programs now being funded and offered, practically no effort is being made to create and implement a better, more future-oriented education for all of our kids.

However well meaning those who propose and fund today's educational reforms may be, their aim is generally to improve something that is obsolete. They are obsessed by the "sit up straight, pay attention, take notes" fantasy of education past. "Discipline" (as opposed to self-discipline, or passion) is heard a lot—Obama used it in his 2010 State of the Union speech. It does not matter how much money these reformers spend; because they are pursuing the wrong goal, their efforts are doomed to failure.

Even if, as result of such efforts, some students achieve better test scores, the current reforms will not solve our real educational problems, which are related not to test scores, but to the future. No matter how innovative programs to improve scores may appear on the surface, it is money being thrown away. If we continue on our current course, we could, in the words of Mark Anderson, "even double or triple the amount being spent, and it wouldn't move the meter one iota."

The tragedy is that if we used the money and momentum now available with the *right* focus and effort, our students' education *could* be made real, valuable, and useful for the future—and fairly easily.

It wouldn't take that much work to decide what should be done—most educators could, I believe, come to consensus. But to get those changes accepted by a majority of our citizens, and to make them actually happen, will require much effort and change on the part of our educational and political leaders. It will also require some new thinking by many, including parents. That is where today's so-called education "reformers"—from Barack Obama to Arne Duncan to Bill Gates to Newt Gingrich—should be, in my opinion, focusing their efforts.

Fix the Education, Not the System

Currently, lots of money is being spent on trying to fix the educational "system." But what the reformers haven't yet understood is that it's not the "system" that we need to get right; *it's the education that the system provides.* This distinction is critical, because one can change almost everything about the "system"—the schools, the leaders, the teachers, the number of hours and days of instruction, and so forth—and still not provide an education that interests our students and gets them deeply engaged in their own learning, or that teaches all of our students what they need to be successful in their 21st century lives.

Unless we change *how* things are taught and *what* is taught, in all of our classrooms, we won't be able to provide an education that has our kids fighting to be *in* school rather than one that effectively pushes one-third to one-half of them out. And this is true for all our kids, both advantaged and disadvantaged.

Most politicians—along with many education reformers—mistakenly believe that our current public school education, designed for an earlier, industrial age, is basically okay, although currently poorly implemented: if we can just find the teachers to teach it right, the thinking goes, and get our students to go through it, they will do better in life as a result. That may once have been the case for most students, but it no longer is. The context, the world, and our kids' educational needs have changed radically, and we need a fresh approach to education.

In part because we "got it right" in the past, the reformers believe that education should remain essentially the same in the lifetimes and careers of today's students as it was in theirs. So the way to fix our current educational issues is to return to what they see as the "funda-mentals" of education: its 20th century incarnation.

Whether couched in terms of values, character building, or behav-iors, and whether or not they allow some contemporary technology to be squeezed in, the reformers fundamentally believe that they can bring back "what once worked." (That it ever worked for all, of course, is a myth.) That belief has tragic ramifications for our students today.

It is tragic *not* because those goals are unimportant for the future. We certainly should preserve, in appropriate quantities, the core val-ues and most useful ideas from the past. It is tragic, rather, because so much of what we do currently teach, and what so many want to pre-serve, is now unimportant because the context for education has changed so radically.

In the current environment, every field and job—from factory work to retail to healthcare to hospitality to garbage collection—is in the process of being transformed dramatically, and often unrecogniz-ably, by technology and other forces. And while most reformers rec-ognize that society is going through dramatic changes (even though few truly "get" their extent, speed, and implications), they too often—and paradoxically—do not see the need for education to change fun-damentally to cope with them.

When politicians, administrators, or even parents believe that succeeding at our current education (i.e., memorizing the multiplica-tion tables, mastering the long division algorithm, being good at paper-book reading, and studying science, history, and civics in tradi-tional ways) is what is important for today's and tomorrow's stu-dents, they put those students at a huge disadvantage relative to the fast-changing future.

When our leaders think that the job of educators is to re-create the old education better and more effectively for today's students, they deny our students the means to cope and thrive in the 21st century. When they think success at education is moving our kids up in the international PISA (Program for International Assessment) rank-ings, they send the message that they want our students to compete in the past.

In other words, the educational medicine most prescribed today—the test-scores-driven, tenure-busting, results-rewarding (in the words of Judith Warner of the *New York Times*) fix of Arne Duncan, Michelle Rhee, and others—will not result in our kids getting the right education, even if it reaches whatever goals they set, because it treats the wrong disease.

Assessment: The Big Gorilla

To deal right away with the "big gorilla" of assessment: I believe that assessment is important, if used correctly, for helping both students and teachers improve. But in the current debate, it leads us away from what we could be doing to actually improve our kids' future.

The much-bandied-about, high-stakes assessments of today are poorly designed, used badly, and give us wrong information. They are poorly designed, despite their claimed statistical sophistication, because they measure things no longer valuable, do not measure many increasingly valuable skills at all, and rely overly on a discredited approach to assessment (i.e., multiple choice questioning). They are used badly because they serve only to rank, and do not provide useful feedback to students and teachers to help them improve. They give wrong information in that they often measure not what kids know, but rather their test-taking abilities.

There are plenty of ways to do assessment differently—and more gently—with much better and more accurate results. For example, Microsoft and other companies are currently at work on assessments that measure student-led learning, as well as assessments that are integrated within the learning process (in ways often similar to how video games assign players "levels" based on accomplishments). Unfortunately, today our high-stakes, standardized testing has become so over-hyped that it is hard to be against such testing and still be for good assessment. The for-profit testing companies, whose executive ranks—perhaps not surprisingly—include many of those who, while in government, pushed the current testing programs, have now become a strong lobby for the current testing regime.

Don't Blame the Teachers (or Students)

Sadly, the biggest consequence of the reformers' false belief that 20th century education can be made to work if only it's better implemented has been the serious, continual, and unwarranted attacks on our two most valuable educational resources: our 55 million students, who *are* our future, and the 3 million adults who courageously choose to teach them. Talk about bullying! These are the people we should be nurturing and helping, rather than beating up.

The failure of the 20th century approach is not the fault of our teachers. While there are clearly some who are not suited to the profession, in the main our 3 million teachers are people of competence and good will. And while there is certainly room for improvement, most are just trying to accomplish, often against their will and better judgment, what the old education asks and mandates of them—that is, to "cover" the curriculum and raise test scores. The teachers I talk to are enormously frustrated by the fact that, while seeing that what they're told to do is not succeeding, they are handcuffed from doing anything else. If we take off those handcuffs and provide a better alternative, most teachers will, I believe, be eager to implement it.

Nor are students to blame for our educational problems. Young people are biologically programmed to always be learning something. The real problem is an education that gives neither the teachers nor the students a chance to succeed. Even if we are successful, as Arne Duncan hopes, in recruiting talented people to replace the 1 million teachers expected to retire, the education model they will be expected to deliver will almost certainly discourage them and beat them down, causing a large percentage to leave.

It also doesn't do our students much good to try to graft lots of "21st century skills" onto existing school programs, while leaving "core" education in place as is—the approach of the Partnership for 21st Century Education, for example. Yes, those skills are important, and adding them is fine, in theory. But unfortunately, our "core" is so overloaded with out-of-date content that it is already impossible to deliver all the things teachers are supposed to in the time they are given. So just adding more skills to the list—even crucial ones—will not work. As I describe later in this essay, we must delete first.

How Much Do Charter Schools Help to Build "21st Century Skills"?

We hear a lot about charters as models of what education in the United States could and should be. But even in that percentage of charter schools and others where the old system *has* been resuscitated—i.e., gotten kids to sit attentively, listening to teachers lecture about the 20th century curriculum—it does little good for our students in the long term. While it may create students who are ready for further advancement in that same system, and it may even get them into college, it does precious little to prepare them for the rest of their lives. In addition, there is no way structurally we could create enough charter schools to replace all our current schools—and college may not be the right goal for every student.

To get to where we want, and need, to go with our children's education, I don't believe that it's necessary to start up thousands of charter schools, creating a new complexity of choices for already confused parents. Doing so would mean struggling with a Herculean task that is basically impossible, and would still leave us with the same problems of providing an appropriate education for today's kids.

The charter schools that *are* "succeeding"—KIPP, Uncommon Schools, and Harlem Zone being a few examples—are essentially succeeding at the old education. That, of course, is what they have to do to be called "successful," because that is all that's measured.

Unfortunately, to succeed in this way, the charters cherry-pick and hire those teachers who are best at the old education, and in doing so, remove those teachers from existing schools. Systematically, the charter approach only shifts things around, and so, in terms of the future, gets us nowhere.

Changing *How* We Teach and *What* We Teach

Rather than start over with new schools, a far better, more effective (and, I believe, easier) approach is to change what goes on in our current classrooms. To change, that is, both *how* we teach and *what* we teach, in ways that reflect our current and future realities.

Changing the "how" means creating a pedagogy that works for today's students. Changing the "what" means creating a curriculum that is future-oriented and engaging to today's students, while remaining useful and rigorous.

Again, the only possible way to accomplish these things is to enlist the competence, skill, and good will of those 3 million teachers we already have, along with those who are entering the profession. We must give these people new directions for what to do and help them do it. Anyone who thinks that teachers can't, or won't, change should look at how quickly they changed their pedagogy to "teaching to the test" after the implementation of No Child Left Behind.

How to Teach—Changing Our Pedagogy to "Partnering"

Changing how we teach for the 21st century means moving to a new, more effective pedagogy—a clear proven pedagogy that I call "partnering" with our students.

"Partnering" is a catchall term for approaches that include problem-based learning, case-based learning, inquiry-based learning, student-centered learning, and others which have until now been seen as "different." At their core, they are all variations on the same central pedagogical idea, generally accepted by experts: *an end to teaching by "telling," and a reassignment of roles for the teacher and students.*

We need to move from the teacher talking and the students taking notes. ("My teachers just talk and talk and talk" is by far the students' biggest complaint about school.) In partnering, the students do what they do—or can do—best, which is finding information, using technology and other resources, and creating. The teachers do what they do best, which is asking the right questions, ensuring quality and rigor, vetting, and adding context and appropriate scaffolding.

This different way of teaching, which has enough variations to be able to be made to work for all our teachers and students, is clear, well thought out, and agreed to by most experts. How to implement it is described in many books (including my own: *Teaching Digital Natives: Partnering for Real Learning*), and it can be done quickly and without changing the curriculum. In its essence, the pedagogy has kids teach themselves, with the coaching and guidance of their teachers.

And, based on the experience of principals and teachers who have used it, partnering is almost certain to lead to higher test scores, because it gets kids far more engaged in their own learning.

This better pedagogy is already being used successfully, under a variety of names (such as "active," "student-centered," "inquiry-based," and "challenge-based" learning), in many of our classrooms. What we need now is to systematically expand its use to *all* existing teachers, subjects, and classes, and to teach it to prospective teachers in our education schools. All this new pedagogy takes to implement is an understanding of how it works, along with a systematic, non-threatening, approach that makes teachers think "I can do this."

We need to refocus our teacher training around more effective pedagogy, rather than just around particular technology tools. In a "verbs versus nouns" metaphor that many find useful, the "verbs" are the unchanging *skills* of education, such as thinking critically, communicating effectively, presenting logically, and calculating correctly. The "nouns" are the *tools* of education—the technologies that students use to learn and practice the skills. In the 21st century, nouns change with increasing rapidity.

For example, for learning the underlying skills (verbs) of presenting, communication, and getting information, nouns (tools) currently used include PowerPoint, email, and Wikipedia. But while the verbs will not change over the course of a student's education, the nouns certainly will. Our pedagogy needs to focus on the underlying verbs, while providing students with, and employing, the best, most up-to-date nouns (tools) to do so—many of which are becoming so inexpensive that they can be supplied to all students at the beginning of each year in most places.

Some of the verbs students need to master are unique to our changing times. Skills like programming digital machines, video communication, statistics, and problem solving should be studied by all our students starting in kindergarten, as we weed out as quickly as possible those skills that are no longer needed—particularly ones that machines can do faster and better.

Currently, far too much emphasis is placed—and training time wasted—on our teachers' learning to use specific nouns, such as blogs or other software. The tools not only change too rapidly for this to be effective, but educationally are best used by students rather than teachers. As important as it is for our children to have access to technology tools, for the tools to be at all effective educationally, the right pedagogy—i.e., the partnering pedagogy—must come first. So it is imperative that we help teachers recognize the benefits of this pedagogy to our students and to themselves, and that we, as a nation, start using it universally.

What to Teach (and What Not to Teach)— Changing Our Curriculum

Changing *what* we teach is probably harder than changing how we teach—not because it is so difficult to figure out, but because the needed changes face so many political and cultural hurdles.

We have an urgent need to create a wholly new curriculum for our 55 million students, retaining the wisdom of the past but reflecting the enormously changed needs of not *only* our 21st century students, but also of their eventual 21st century employers.

But because our curricula are already overstuffed, the new curriculum must begin with deletion—figuring out and eliminating those things that are no longer truly needed, yet take up tremendous amounts of class time. Since every piece of our current curriculum has its backers and partisans, it is crucial that everyone be made to understand this need to delete, or we will never make progress. To those who maintain that students should take years of 1,000-year-old geometry because it helps their logical thinking, we must respond: "So does programming, and it will help them get jobs."

Deletion candidates in elementary school, for example, include cursive handwriting, the long division algorithm, and—very controversially—memorization of the multiplication tables. Deletion candidates in higher grades include much (though certainly not all) of some traditional mathematics courses and many details of history (not the broad strokes, of course).

I am not suggesting that we totally abandon all these once-useful things, many of which are dear to the hearts of educators and parents. But it is time to put them on the reference shelf, alongside the Latin and Greek we once required, for retrieval only when and if needed by particular students.

I strongly believe that if we are able to change these two things— how we teach and what we teach in our current classrooms—our current and future teachers, with some training, are fully capable of delivering, and will deliver, the education our students so desperately need.

Steps in the Right Direction

Despite all the focus that reformers place on testing, our hardest and most pressing educational problem is not raising test scores, but rather connecting our kids' education to real life and to the fast-evolving world of the future. It is our inability to make the material we are currently required to teach in school *real* and *interesting* for today's students—call it relevance, or engagement, or something else— that makes so many current efforts unsuccessful. And our teachers know it.

We must, first and fundamentally, re-design education to be con- nected to students' "reality"—the world they see and know. While stu- dents have always asked "Why should I learn this?" the answer, for most things, is now less and less clear. The real reason kids have to learn most of what they are taught today is "because it's in the curriculum," not because it will be useful long term. (This could be easily verified by having adults take the SATs and making their scores public.)

In the words of Angus King, the former governor of Maine, "Our kids should sue us for the education they now get." Similarly, David Engle, school superintendent and U.S. program director for Project Inkwell, has said: "Every student is damaged or cheated out of a more productive future by our continued adherence to an old, defunct system design."

Ignoring Students' Passions at Our Peril

And it gets worse. Current U.S. education ignores almost entirely the thing that has always been America's greatest strength: the passion of our people.

Amazingly, our current education places no importance on even knowing the individual passions, or interests, of our students, and most teachers don't ask—not necessarily because they don't care, but because they are so occupied with all the other required tasks (such as teaching for the tests) that they feel they have no time. But if we lack the time to find out who our students really are and what they like, it is hard to create an education that interests them.

Although we have been moving the deck chairs of "system" reform for some time now, we are still at the very beginning of even *thinking* about the "right" education and curriculum for our students, in terms of how and what we teach.

To better employ the greater amounts of time that deletion will enable (years, perhaps!), we can add much-needed, and currently largely untaught, behaviors and skills, including proper online behavior and etiquette, controlling our increasingly complex machines (e.g., programming), understanding and correctly using statistics (especially polling statistics), literacy in non-textual and mixed media, systematic problem solving, using technology to effect change, and the basics of communication in all the world's major languages— all beginning in the earliest grades and continuing throughout all the school years. Changing the curriculum in this way is just in its infancy, but the need is urgent.

Everything we teach should also be matched with a clear answer to the student's constant question of "Why am I learning this?" Students should be taught to immediately use what they learn to effect outcomes in the world, and change it for the better. For example, they can use their learning to design a school of the future, or to redesign their current school. They can use the languages they learn to work directly with foreign students. They can learn to perform professional energy and environmental audits of local businesses. They can use their knowledge and skills to create Public Service Announcements for local TV and radio stations.

The 3 P's

To those who argue that patience and delayed gratification are important, I answer yes, but only if students are convinced their efforts will truly pay off in ways that are important to them. It is therefore crucial that we create a curriculum that is focused almost exclusively on future reality, and on connections to today's and tomorrow's world, while respecting the past.

The new curriculum should be much more cross-disciplinary and integrated than is currently the case, because this is how the world works. Additionally, it needs to focus much of its teaching on at least three areas that are not given enough—or often any—systematic attention in our current education. Let's call them the "3 P's": Passion (including character), Problem Solving (including communication), and Producing what is required, with creativity and skill. In the new curriculum, all subjects would be taught in the context of these 3 P's, rather than just being grafted onto an existing content base. To elaborate:

Passion and Character

Systematically focusing on passion and character will correct one of our current education's greatest failings: focusing more on content and subjects than on the people being educated.

In the current system—or at least the public portion, which is most of it—there is an almost total lack of curricular emphasis on character, i.e., becoming a good person in addition to a good student. Teachers may work on this, but it is not "in the curriculum," except in the earliest grades. When our current education was conceived, such character education was mostly left to the home and family, a context that no longer exists sufficiently (or in some cases not at all) for many of our students. We need to find ways of making character a cornerstone of our education, while still maintaining the secular values that characterize public education. Here is one place we can look to some of our private and charter school successes for guidance.

The formal part of our education has also almost totally excluded our students' passions. Some of these passions get to be expressed in extracurricular activities, but students will do far better if their personal passions can be more integrated into our teaching. Students often complain that too many of their teachers don't know them as individuals. At the least, all our teachers should know what their students' passions are and help those students approach their school subjects through the lens of those passions.

Problem Solving and Communication

Communication and problem solving are highly linked: most 21st century problem solving is done in groups, and even the best of solutions are worthless when not shared. Yet we currently do not approach either communication or problem solving systematically and holistically in all subjects.

I believe that almost every problem in life can be helpfully viewed (and many solved) through the lens of a common framework, a framework that we should teach to all students, from kindergarten to college. This "Five Skills Framework for Problem Solving" can be seen in detail at www.marcprensky.com/writing/framework, and is the subject of my upcoming book, *Problem-Solving, Passion, and Producing the Right Stuff.* The Five Skills Framework, if applied to all subjects, would create thousands of new problem-solving and communication experiences over the course of an education, and become a useful tool in students' 21st century lives. The five problem-solving skills are:

1. Figuring Out the Right (or Best) Thing to Do

2. Getting It Done

3. Working With Others

4. Doing It Creatively

5. Continually Doing It Better

Each skill is further broken down into supporting skills. For example, "Figuring Out the Right (or Best) Thing to Do" includes Identifying Problems, Behaving Ethically, Thinking Critically, Making Good Decisions and Judgments, and Setting Goals.

Producing What Is Required, With Creativity and Skill

Creativity, as several educational observers these days have noted, is often actively *dis*couraged in our current education. Given the tools that our students have increasing access to—many right in their pockets—with enormous capabilities and power that were only dreamed about in the past, today's students ought to be the most creative in history. Our future curriculum and education should be about unleashing all our students' creativity with these tools, in every subject and in every area of student passion.

Again, it is not the tools themselves that we need to focus on, but rather the products, creativity, and skills that the tools enable and enhance.

Appropriate Education for All Students

American tradition holds that it is important to educate everybody, and I am in total agreement. All of our students need these changes.

Paradoxically, the success of some of our students with the old education distracts many observers and sends them down the wrong path, because it holds out the false hope that if only our schools did a better job of what we currently ask of them (i.e., if only there were a teacher with a master's degree in every classroom, for example, or longer school hours, or tighter discipline), then the existing system could be fixed for everyone.

Those students who succeed in the long run, *despite* an education that is largely out-of-date, do so because they have the internal means. We should be striving to give all of our students a far better education, with skills and challenges that prepare them for the future. While also doing far better for our brightest students, we must focus equally—or even more—on the perhaps more challenging problem of what to do for those 90 percent of students who are *not* in the very top percentiles.

While our top students often go on to get further education to make up for what they've missed, the other 90 percent, because they often don't have the ability or means to get another education somewhere else, rely on their public education as their only hope. They see their expected jobs disappearing, and they are afraid.

The Importance of Asking the Right Questions

While a great many well-meaning people in government, philanthropy, and business have recently noticed our educational problems and have rushed into action, most have failed to ask the right questions.

Is the right solution to the hyper-changing world to push all students up to college, or to match their education with the needs of emerging jobs? Is the right solution to kids' falling behind to demonize their schools and teachers with poor rankings, or to find ways to help each student individually? Is the right solution to America's falling behind in comparisons to catch up on the statistics, or to take a different route to success? Is the right solution to the high number of dropouts to discipline our kids into getting an old education or to incentivize them into getting a new one? Is the right way to get kids to attend our schools to pay them (as some suggest), or to create an education that they fight to get into? Is the right way to spend our money and creative efforts to start or expand more charter schools, or to change what goes on in all our existing classrooms?

When leaders and reformers diagnose the *problem* wrongly (i.e., as the need to patch up, rather than completely reform, the old education), they choose the wrong solutions and actions to fix it. Why has this happened? One possible reason is that practically all of the leaders and reformers—whatever their ideology—received the old education themselves, and then succeeded in life. They may believe that since that education worked for them, it can work for everyone. But using oneself as a sole data point is one of the most elementary mistakes in reasoning.

A second reason is that many believe the old education is the "right" education, constructed around basics they perceive as "timeless." But only a very few of the basic skills a person needs are truly timeless—most depend heavily on environment and context. The basics of yesterday or today—decoding squiggles, fine cursive penmanship, calculations on paper—are not going to be the basics of tomorrow or forever. Already, in the 21st century, a great many of these old "basics" have been offloaded to personal machines such as watches, calculators, cell phones, and computers, which should, ideally, leave our children's minds available for more tasks at higher levels.

Why Business-Based Education Solutions Have Been Missing the Mark

A great deal of the blame for today's wrong-headed approach to fixing our education lies, I believe, with the recent influx of businesspeople and "business thinking" into education and educational reform.

In New York City, for example—America's largest school district—the mayor, who is a businessman, wrested control of the educational system (possibly a good thing), but then installed a businessman to run his schools. After that person's seven years, the education of New York City's kids, despite some tiny pilots, is hardly more oriented to the future than before. And when that businessman's tenure was over, the mayor turned to another businessperson, whom he chose because she is, in his words, a "superstar manager." (That lasted three months.)

What these people are expected to bring to education is, of course, business management ideas, and they do—so much so, in fact, that I watch in amazement the amount of money now being spent on things like "improving school management," "accountability," and "leadership," rather than on improving our students' education. Why? Because that is what businesspeople know (although, as I learned as a student at Harvard Business School, business management can be a seat-of-the-pants, make-it-up-as-you-go art).

Don't get me wrong: it's not my opinion that school management, accountability, and leadership aren't important—they are. But they are far from the crux of education, or of our educational problem. That problem is to change what goes on every day in every classroom in America; to change what we teach and how we teach it. Businesspeople, unfortunately, have few useful ideas on how to do this. In fact, their ideas have led mainly to our schools' increasingly viewing students as fungible products whose quality is measured only by test scores.

Business managers coming into education focus mainly on the behavior of their employees, typically giving short shrift to the opinions of the kids who are getting the education. They bring in all the latest management tools and fads (management has even more fads than education does!) and repeat a largely irrelevant-to-education mantra of "Accountability, Measurement, Data," as if that might fix what is wrong in our classrooms. They spend enormous amounts of our limited and precious educational resources on systems to collect, compile, and analyze huge quantities of information, insisting that all educational decisions be data-driven. Never mind that the data they measure is often inappropriate for the real educational goals, that what they hold people accountable for is typically wrongly defined, or that they are training leaders to lead in the wrong direction.

A school may be "better run" if it has an effective leader, but it will not necessarily offer students a better education. The educational changes truly needed to do that will come not from better superintendents or principals, but—again—from changes in how and what we teach.

While administrators can encourage this, they cannot make it happen. The only thing that will make the needed changes happen in sufficient numbers is a bottoms-up appreciation and recognition by teachers of the need for, and adoption of, new approaches. And that will happen only when reformers create and effectively promote such approaches.

Sadly, what the influx of business thinking has mostly brought to education is our current destructive over-testing, and the poor pedagogy of teaching to the test. It has also led, I believe, to a huge gap in the types of educational innovations truly needed, and to an increasingly bleak future for our kids.

Curriculum Overload and the Need to Delete

To be fair, there have been some positive attempts by businesspeople to identify new skills needed for future business jobs—particularly through the Partnership for 21st Century Skills, a consortium of business companies. But unfortunately, even this work, while helpful in many respects, avoids the most important issue regarding students' actual learning of the new skills.

Merely identifying the necessary skills is not the key task, nor even the most difficult one; many observers have figured these out. Again: the greater difficulty is, rather, that teachers cannot just add these skills onto what they already teach (as the Partnership suggests), because the current curricula are so overloaded.

The truly hard work, which hasn't been forthcoming from the business sector, is figuring out what skills can be deleted from the curricula, with little or no loss, in order to make room for the new. Admittedly, deleting is much more controversial than adding. But by not recommending and supporting specific deletions, business managers have essentially punted, which has handed the tough task of making room for the new skills, and getting them taught and learned effectively, back to the educators.

So, unfortunately, the business sector has not provided the answer to our educational problems or needs. The only way to change education is to change our expectations for what should happen in all our classrooms, and to empower our teachers and students to make it happen.

The Real Culprit:
Stealthy Resistance to Forward Movement

To reiterate: the biggest impediment to a better education for our children is the often deeply rooted belief that education needs to move backwards: back to "disappearing values," back to kids with "longer attention spans," back to "teachers who stood up and really taught." At a time when the world is moving forward at hyper-speed, this makes little sense.

The proposition that "more education inevitably leads to success" has also become common wisdom among politicians, parents, and others, because, until not long ago, it was true that, statistically speaking, getting through school paid off, big time. Historically, the further one got in the system, the better one did: averages from past years show large lifetime advantages in earning power for those earning bachelor's or master's degrees.

But unfortunately, the statistics of the past are no guarantee for our children's future. Past statistics are reliable predictors *only if conditions remain roughly the same*—and in the case of education and jobs, almost everything is changing radically. The world will continue to change even faster as our students grow up; and in this environment of hyper-change, all bets are off.

Remember how many people believed (based largely on past data) that housing prices would always go up—until they fell? The only way to ensure that the positive link between more education and better jobs applies in the 21st century is to make major changes to the education we give our students.

Only the *Right* Education Helps

Again, please understand—I am a firm believer in education as a way to get ahead. I very much agree that getting the right education, and as much of it as possible, will help all students in life. But I do not believe that what we currently offer our students *is* the right education for their future.

Since all the important changes we need will take time, what can we do for our 55 million kids in the meantime? How can we make their current learning real and engaging for them, and not a waste of their time, causing one-quarter of them or more to walk out the door before graduating from high school? For me, this requires a short-term laser focus on the "how we teach"—i.e., on changing our pedagogy.

Our current education forces teachers to apply their efforts in misguided directions that sap their energy and effectiveness. I believe that there are an enormous number of teachers who would do a much better job if they were allowed to ensure the learning of the key parts of whatever subject they teach, rather than being required to "cover" the entire detailed curriculum of their subject or grade level—and if they were not burdened by the kinds and amounts of high-stakes testing now required. If our kids are to learn, we need to release, not destroy, our teachers' creative energy.

Focus on the Kids

Just as we need to liberate and empower our teachers, we need to do the same for our students. Our current education is frequently demeaning and disrespectful, too often unnecessarily subordinating the individual needs and desires of students to those of the system.

In the teacher hiring process, there are many requirements for "degrees earned," but few, if any, for "empathy with students." Unbelievably, our educational system neither teaches nor tells teachers directly that the most important part of their job is *connecting with students*, not delivering content.

Those (many) teachers who do connect deeply with students typically find that they're out on their own. Still, given all the other pressures the system puts on them to cover the curriculum and prepare students for tests, few are able to connect profoundly with enough of their students, and this is something our educators should both require and facilitate.

"Easy to Do/Big Impact" Steps

If, tomorrow, every teacher in America spent 20 minutes of class time asking each student what her or his passion was, and then later used that information to understand each student more deeply and differentiate their instruction accordingly, education would take giant positive steps forward overnight.

It is actions like this—steps that take minimal time and effort on the part of teachers, but have great potential positive impact on kids' education—that we should be looking for to improve education in the short term, even as we work to reform it in the longer term.

Other "easy to do/big impact" steps include:

- Less "telling" by teachers (and allowing kids to research the answers to guiding questions on their own);
- Always connecting what is taught with real-world outcomes;
- Helping students distinguish the unchanging "verbs" (skills) of education from the rapidly changing "nouns" (tools);
- Treating students as learning partners;
- Employing students' own tools (particularly video and cell phones) for learning;
- Using more peer-to-peer teaching;
- Offering students far more choices, rather than mandating what all must read or do;
- Allowing students to be the primary users (and maintainers) of classroom technology;
- Sharing of successes via short videos posted on sites such as YouTube or TeacherTube; and
- Regularly connecting students with the world via free, secure tools such as Skype and ePals.

Conclusion

It is sad for our children, and America's future, that we are so focused on re-creating and fixing the past. Our children deserve a 21st century education, one that prepares them not just for the day they leave school, but for their future careers and the rest of their lives.

Certainly, all of today's students should be able to read and write at some minimum level. But it is equally certain that those skills will be far less important in most of our kids' lifetimes than they are today, as new core skills take their place. Without the changes to our goals and focus described here, our government's much-hyped "Race to the Top" is nothing but a race back to the 20th century.

I would caution those who might dismiss the ideas in this piece as just another incarnation of approaches that have been tried in the past and failed. "Some might see this," says James Paul Gee, professor of Literacy Studies at Arizona State,

> as just recycling project-based and other old progressive approaches, while failing to deal with the issues of standards that has bedeviled these approaches. But, in fact, this is not about old-style progressive approaches. It is about immersion in doing that is still well-structured by good design, about mentorship, and about resourcing from teachers and peers. It is about assessment that can be done inside learning all along and not just at the end in some "drop out of the sky test." It is a call for a fresh approach to 21st century education in America that is desperately needed.

America's rankings in the PISA scores, along with the fact that China and India have more honors students than the United States has students, are often cited to support a need for America to catch up. But at Harvard Business School I learned that when competing with such giants, it is far better to have a different, more clever, strategy than to just work harder at doing the same thing they do.

There is no point to our competing with the Chinese or Indians (or Finns or Singaporeans) on test scores—we should let them win (and brag about) those useless comparisons of the past.

America should be building, rather, on our unique strengths, focusing our main efforts and resources not on book learning from the past and standardized testing, but on stimulating the passion and creativity of all our young people, and on honing our well-deserved reputation for ingenuity and entrepreneurship. If we do this—and do it right—our young people will flock back into our schools, and the America of the future will remain the envy of the world.

2

On Learning

(Original title: "E-Nough")

"e-Learning" is a misnomer—it's mostly just "e-Teaching." For *any* teaching to reliably and consistently produce the results we want, we still have a lot to learn about learning.

Published in On the Horizon

I wrote this essay early on, when I first began to re-examine education and learning. There was much hoopla at that time about "e-Learning"—the term had just come into wide use. But even though much of it was available, it was unclear how much it was helping students (if at all) and under what conditions. So I began looking at learning, and I was appalled at what I found— despite thousands of years of people doing it, learning was still poorly understood. Not just at the neurological level, which we have only gotten to recently, but at the behavioral level—what caused learning, what prevented it, and what could make it better. All we really had, I found, were lots of often-conflicting theories, most of which were aimed at learning as classes, not as individuals. So I tried here to clarify the situation, in the hope of improving it.

☙ ☙ ❧ ❧

*I'm always ready to learn,
although I do not always like being taught.*

—Winston Churchill

What is learning? Are there different kinds? How many? Can we accurately measure them? Can we produce them reliably? How long do they last?

These perennially important learning questions are newly relevant in the context of "electronic teaching." *The trouble is, we have no good answers to any of them.* But we do know one thing—teaching ("e" or otherwise) does not guarantee learning.

What *Is* Learning, Anyway?

Although the two are often conflated, teaching and learning are very different—teaching is done *to* people, in open view; learning is done *by* people and happens in the privacy and solipsistic isolation of each student's mind.

It is fashionable in some circles today to say "everybody learns differently." And in one sense this is completely true—we all come to whatever it is to be learned with different experiences, all of which affect our learning. ("Prior knowledge" and "g"—the general intelligence factor[1]—are the two most important factors influencing learning.) Yet we are also all humans, with the same biology. And learning is a biological process. So how do we reconcile these two things when we design our "e-Teaching"?

"Learning theory" has moved historically from learning as something unknowable (philosophy), to learning as something knowable only indirectly through behavior (psychology), to learning as something that will someday be as well-understood as the process of digestion (neuroscience). "Everything the brain produces, from the most private thoughts to the most public acts, should be understood as a biological process," writes Nobel-Prize-in-Medicine-winning scientist Eric R. Kandel in the chapter "Cellular Mechanisms of Meaning and the Biological Basis of Individuality" in the standard textbook

Principles of Neural Science (4th ed. 2000). Many today think about an over-arching multi-discipline of "Cognitive Science."

So we might wonder "What have all these scientists discovered that can help us build better learning programs?" So far, not as much as we would like, it turns out. For they have still not produced definitive consensus on what learning is, how many kinds there are, how we produce and measure them, and how long the effects last.

Why We Know So Little

I'm going to suggest at least three reasons for this. First, we don't always ask (or answer) the right questions about learning, or make the right distinctions. Second, our efforts to quickly direct research toward improving classroom teaching often lead us astray. And third, there are some old concepts and language that are just very difficult for us to throw away, along with some old common-sense truths that are very hard for many to accept.

Despite researchers' supposed "open minds" it is surprising how often key questions—especially ones that are tough to answer—are excluded from being asked. Stephen Wolfram cites mathematics as a discipline which routinely defines those questions it can't answer as being "outside the field." "What is learning?" ranks high among these rarely asked—and certainly unsatisfactorily answered—questions.

Since one job of the teaching profession is to assess learning, one might assume that anyone in the teaching profession could easily define precisely what learning is, and that all their answers would be essentially the same. But I doubt it. (Go to the Web right now and email me your own answer to "What is learning?"—without looking anything up—at marc@games2train.com. We'll see just how much consensus there actually is.)

I suspect that one of the basic reasons we have made such little process in assessing students' learning is that we lack a good understanding of what learning really is. We often don't even define it. The recently published book *How People Learn*, for example (National Academy Press 2000), a report of the Committee on Developments in the Science of Learning of the Commission on Behavior and Social Science of the National Research Council, with additional material from the Committee on Learning Research and Educational Practice (!), never defines the "what" for which they claim to have "explained" the "how."

Can *anyone* define learning?

"Although learning can be understood as a change in an organism's capacities or behavior brought about by experience," writes Daniel Riesberg in the entry "Learning" in the MIT cognitive sciences online database (http://cognet.mit.edu/MITECS/Entry/reisberg.html), "this rough definition encompasses many cases usually not considered examples of learning (e.g., an increase in muscular strength brought about by exercise). More important," he goes on, "it fails to reflect the many forms of learning which may be distinguished, for example, according to what is learned, may be governed by different principles, and may involve different processes."

Note Riesberg's heavy use of the conditional: *May* be distinguished, *may* be governed, *may* involve. We really don't know.

How can this be? How can it be that the very core mechanism of what we are trying to do remains an indefinable mystery? If we can't say what it is we're trying to produce, how can we judge if we are producing it, and doing it right, or in the best way? In fact how can we judge if we are doing it at all?

If you think these questions are frivolous, think again. For we are, I maintain, with respect to learning, pretty much where medicine was in the 18th century. They knew and could recognize the result they wanted to produce: a healthy body. We are trying to produce an educated, trained or "learned" person. Like those early doctors, we have a few means that have worked reliably in some situations over millennia.

But just try to get consensus on exactly what works when and with whom. In most of our learning situations, we are at sea. As we will see in a minute, there is absolutely no agreement on the "right" way to produce learning, with any group, in any situation, at any level. We move from fad to fad. If something works in one place, educators tend to just apply it all over, just like those 18th century doctors who "bled" their patients for any ailment. I imagine someone once or twice must have seen a healing result that correlated with a bleeding. But an awful lot of people were bled to death—George Washington among them! Although our primitive knowledge of learning may not have actually killed anybody (has it?), many of us have suffered harm at the hands of people trying to make learning happen, and many of us in turn continue to turn around and inflict the same harm on our students.

So let's consider the question "What is learning?" Is it one thing? Is it several things? If the latter, why do we use the same word?

The people from educational research, educational methods, pedagogy, instructional design, learning science, cognition and instruction, cognitive psychology, behavioral psychology, educational psychology, human factors, training, child development, linguistics, neuro-linguistics, biology, computer science, neuroscience, and cognitive neurology, don't have a clear answer. In fact, the National Academy of Science (NAS) has established a committee on "New Development in the Science of Learning," whose goal is to "synthesize new findings from research to create a user-friendly theory of human learning."

Unfortunately, they haven't yet produced one, at least not for public consumption. But the sooner they get there the better. What we now have are *lots* of theories—hundreds, in fact. If you care to, you can read about many of them in the *Handbook of Contemporary Learning Theories* (Mowrer & Klein, eds., Lawrence Erlbaum Assoc. 2000) and at the TIP database, where 52 [now 54] of them are listed in alphabetical order, from "ACT*" through "Triarchic" (http://tip.psychology.org/theories.html). And you'll have to go yet elsewhere for neurological-based theories.

Why is there so little attempt to do what physics does, for example—unite all these partial theories ("theorettes"?) into a larger coherent theory and not be satisfied until we do? After all, the brain functions the same way (although perhaps not equally effectively) in all of us, despite our individual differences in prior knowledge, "g," and other things. Whatever the processes that constitute learning, they have to be the same at their core for everyone. What are they? How many different key pieces are there? How do they fit together?

Defining Learning

The dictionary defines learning as "gaining knowledge or skill" (*Concise Oxford Dictionary* 1999).

Psychologists define learning as "a relatively permanent change in behavior that is attributable to practice and experience, inferred from improvement in performance" [http://www.wpunj.edu/cos/ex-movsci/mllearn/sld001.htm].

Neuroscientists teach that "learning is the process by which we acquire knowledge about the world, while memory is the process by which that knowledge is encoded, stored, and later retrieved" [*Principles of Neural Science,* Kandel, Schwartz, & Jessell, 4th ed. 2000].

Let me propose a definition of my own:

Human Learning is the set of processes people employ, both consciously and unconsciously, to effect changes to their knowledge, capacities, and/or beliefs.

Whatever its failings, this definition helps us remember that: (1) Learning is not one process, but several—sometimes separate, often interrelated. These processes can be enumerated, and associated with material to be learned. (2) Learning must be done by the learner—whether consciously or unconsciously—it can't be done by a teacher or anyone else. (3) Learning involves not only "knowledge" (facts, groups of facts, relationships between facts), and "doing" (capacities tasks, skills and behaviors) but also "beliefs" (theories, understanding of how and why things work or happen), which are much less often talked about in this context. What this definition *leaves out* is also important: "acquisition" "experience" "permanence" "improvement" "performance," and especially "being taught" are not intrinsic to learning, although they are related.

The Great "How Do People Learn" Debate

Of course having a definition is hardly enough—we need to know *how* people learn. Today asking that question is a lot like asking "What is the true religion?" Every religious person is convinced his or her religion is the true one, and yet there are, according to one organization that tracks them, over 4,000 different religions in the world.[2] We may not have thousands of learning theories, but we do have hundreds. Instead of a coherent understanding, what we have at the turn of the second millennium—after dealing with learning for literally thousands of years—is just a large variety of points of view on how learning happens, each with its own self-proclaimed experts, each with a particular "theorette" of learning to champion. Let's look at some examples:

Learning comes from doing.

Learning is imitation, which is unique to man and a few animals.

You can't learn unless you fail.

Learning happens when one is engaged in hard and challenging activities.

Learning comes from observing people we respect.

Learning is a developmental process.

Learning is primarily a social activity.

Learning needs multiple senses involved.

Learning happens best without thinking.

Learning happens better by thinking about it.

Learning takes practice, says one. No, says another, that's "drill and kill."

People learn in context. People learn when elements are *abstracted* from context.

We learn by principles, says one. By procedures, says the other.

They can't *think,* says the one. They can't *add,* says the other.

Everyone has a different "learning style."

We learn X percent of what we hear, Y percent of what we see, Z percent of what we do.

Situated learning, says one. Case-based reasoning, says another. Goal-based learning, says a third. All of the above, says a fourth.

Learning should be fun, peeps the girl in the corner. Learning is hard work, answers another.

We learn automatically, from the company we keep, says yet another.

People learn in "chunks."

People learn just in time, only when they need to.

People learn aurally, visually, and kinesthetically.

People learn through feedback.

People learn through reflection.

People learn through a loop of doing and reflecting.

People learn through coaching.

People learn from constructing things.

People learn from models.

People learn from mistakes.

People learn from stories and parables.

People learn by constructing their own knowledge.

People learn when they're working.

People learn by playing.

People learn through games.

People learn when they're having fun.

People learn in context.

People learn when things are relevant.

And on, and on, and on.

How can we have such disparity? Is learning really that complicated? I strongly suspect it's not. In my opinion researchers have complicated matters related to learning *so far* beyond where they need to be in order for us to understand and use them, that it has rendered the entire body of learning research practically useless. No wonder the NAS wants to create "a 'user-friendly' theory of human learning."

Do we need *more* research? In their book *The Monster Under the Bed*, Stan Davis and Jim Bodkin point out that nationally, "less than 0.1 percent [yes, that's one-tenth of one percent] of our school budgets is destined for educational research—the lowest figure for research spent on any major budgeted activity. Compared with health, defense, space, energy or new products, new knowledge on the learning process is definitely a poor relation. . . . The federal government spends three times more for agricultural research, twenty-one times more for space research, and 30 times more for research on health." "We know more about how to improve the use of diapers," they say, "than of brains."[3]

But the real issue may not be quantity so much as quality. "The history of educational research is not necessarily encouraging to those who foresee a golden age of scientific clarity," writes James Traub in the *New York Times*.[4] There *is* a lot of stuff out there branded as "learning research." But as anyone who has ever looked at it knows, most of it is not just user-unfriendly—it's also full of opinion, conjecture, and wishful thinking that is partly or totally incorrect. "People outside of the educational establishment are often shocked to learn how little in instructional practice has been evaluated using the standard paraphernalia of social science-control groups, random assignment, data collection, statistics," writes MIT psychology professor Steven Pinker.[5] And much of the best research, done inside the armed forces for training purposes, rarely if ever gets looked at outside the military.

Further, although much of the research conflates learning with education and pedagogy, it still has little connection to classroom practice, which, says Pinker, "is set by fads, romantic theories, slick packages and political crusades."

How can this happen?

A great part of the reason is that there is so little theoretical consensus—scientific or otherwise—about what learning is and how to make it happen. And one key reason for this is that there is so little differentiation in the term "learning."

Learning Differentiation

One possible explanation for so many competing theories of how people learn is that "learning" is an extremely broad term, covering a lot of ground. Riesberg (above) tells us there are "many forms of learning which may be distinguished, for example, according to what is learned, may be governed by different principles, and may involve different processes." The standard neuroscience textbook says that "From a cognitive point of view, any complex human activity almost always involves an intricate interplay among different kinds of knowledge, perceptual discriminations, motor and cognitive skills, strategies and performance demands or contexts. Correspondingly, many kinds of learning are involved, and they are not all achieved in the same way." Christine Massey of the Institute for Cognitive Research at the University of Pennsylvania says there is a need for "more differentiated views of learning."

The key issue here is differentiating between the various "types" of learning. We are deeply in need of more and better distinctions between such things as:

- The learning that goes on constantly, 24/7—mostly, but not entirely, at a non-conscious level—just because we are human and take things in. (Take a university course on the first day. Before I hear a word the teacher says, I have learned much from and about her, including approximate age, sex, posture, attitude, punctuality, and possibly the part of the world her ancestors came from. As she talks I am learning about her speech, clarity of thought, many more attitudes (nice, mean, etc.), style (formal or informal). I'm learning about my classmates from the way they react to him and to each other. I'm learning about the ventilation in the room, and possibly, from the smells around me, what some people had (or are having) for lunch.

- The learning of "information," such as when I learn the name of my teacher, the names of my classmates, and what texts we will be using. I learn what the teacher says, at least in the sense that I have heard it (consciously or not), and possibly written it down. Professors in medicine and the sciences know that this kind of learning (or rather the fact it exists in your mind) may sometimes get recalled unexpectedly in times of need, as in "I seem to remember one of my teachers talking about that once when I was half asleep. . . . "
- The learning when we give something our full consciousness and attention. This consists of both taking in information and making various connections in our head with other information.
- The learning where we transfer things from short- to long-term memory, as, for example when we learn new vocabulary.
- The learning where we discover principles that we can articulate and then apply in other situations.
- The conscious, step-by-step learning of skills or procedures.
- The learning that transfers skills consciously learned into non-conscious behaviors through repeated practice (such as in surgery).
- The learning of skills that are hard or impossible to put into words, such as riding a bicycle or juggling.
- The combination of conscious and non-conscious learning of new abilities, such as writing, or interpersonal skills.
- The learning from playing with systems, simulations, and other participatory experiences.
- The learning in debriefings and after action reviews.

And this is by no means the definitive or exhaustive list.

For something so central to what we do, our learning vocabulary is extremely impoverished. The few distinctions and names we have are inconsistent. Some distinguish between "knowledge, skills, and abilities," others between "hard" skills and "soft" skills. Knowledge is classified by some as Explicit versus Implicit, by others as Declarative versus Non-declarative, by still others as Tacit, Conditionalized or Inert. Neuroscientists speak of declarative memory and non-declarative memory, the latter including priming, procedural, associative, and non-associative. Some refer to learning as "reflexive" or "reflective," others to "artisan" and "virtuoso" learners. All this is not terribly helpful, because there is such different usage and so much crossover. Are we talking about the same things? Do we have the "cuts" right? Why can't we all just come to consensus?

At this point I'm not yet proposing a new vocabulary list. But I am suggesting we would all benefit from thinking more about this question.

One key differentiator mentioned above but often ignored is *what* is being learned—not particular subject matter content, but the *type* of material (facts, judgment, theory, etc.). It is useful because it leads us directly to different types of learning. For example, a budding doctor in medical school needs to learn the English and Latin names of all the parts of the body (facts), the ways the body systems behave (theory, observation, dynamics), how to perform procedures (physical skills), how to diagnose (process, judgment, reason), how to talk with patients and manage time (behavior, skill), how to present cases to other doctors (language), and how to do research (organization, discovery), among many other things. Each of these requires a different type of learning.

But we rarely, if ever, hear "these are ways that people learn *facts.* And these are ways that people learn *skills.* And these are ways that people learn *theory.* And these are the ways people learn *judgment.* And these are ways that people learn to *reason.*" When we do this, many of our problems in creating learning—with or without technology—begin to sort themselves out, because we know, from long experience, how most of these types of learning happen:

We learn *facts* through questions, memorization, association, and drill.

We learn *skills (physical or mental)* through imitation, feedback, continuous practice, and increasing challenge.

We learn *judgment* through hearing stories, asking questions and making choices, and getting feedback and coaching.

We learn *behaviors* through imitation, feedback, and practice.

We learn *processes* through observation, explanation, and practice.

We learn *about existing theories* through logical explanation and questioning.

We learn to *create and test theories* through experimentation and questioning.

We learn *reasoning* through puzzles and examples.

We lean *procedures* through imitation and practice.

We learn *creativity* through playing.

We learn *language* through imitation, practice, and immersion.

We learn *programming and other systems* through principles and graduated tasks.

We learn *observation* through examples, doing, and feedback.

We learn *speeches or performance roles* by memorization, practice, and coaching.

We learn *the behavior of dynamic systems* by observation and experimentation.

This list is by no means complete or exhaustive, but is meant to show only that the same learning methods are not used for every type of thing we learn. In every discipline or domain there are a wide variety of materials or content to be learned by students, all of which *are* learned differently.

So the best first cut on understanding learning, it seems to me, is not by type of learner, or subject matter, *but by type of material to be learned.* The second cuts are more individualistic—what does this person already know, and how "smart" is he or she?

Without these differentiations in learning we cannot truly understand what is going on in the learning process or how to make it happen. Too often our so-called "learning experts" fail to take these types of distinctions into account, and speak of learning as if it were a single, monolithic process. "People learn by X," they say, or "People don't learn by Y." But not a single one of these blanket statements is true. We don't learn *everything* by "doing" or "failure" or "reflection" or anything else. It's a mix we have to sort out. And by *not* sorting, the so-called "experts" lead us astray.

"Herding"

How else do the so-called "learning experts" lead us astray? The insistence of many on a limited number of "learning styles" based on such things as a "written, oral, or kinesthetic" predilection or "multiple intelligences" or Myers-Briggs classifications, etc. (often based on little or no evidence) is leading us seriously down false paths, especially in creating e-Teaching.

But even more destructive, in my view, is that in a rush to "apply" the results of learning research to education and teaching, researchers often wind up making it harder for us to understand what is happening with individual learners. Designers of electronic teaching who do not have backgrounds in "education," "instructional design," "pedagogy," or "cognitive psychology" (but come at the issue of creating learning as a pragmatic problem in need of solution) often find the so-called "learning experts'" work almost totally useless. I have often wondered why this is so, and I finally think I have figured it out. While some researchers *do* study learning to find out how it works, the groups mentioned above study learning principally to "improve education." ("Applied" research.) And since most of our education happens in groups (i.e., classes), what they are really trying to figure out is "how learning happens in groups." Unfortunately, learning doesn't happen in groups at all—learning happens in minds. And minds are helped best to learn in a one-on-one situation.

It has been absolutely clearly and firmly established (to a large extent, but not exclusively, by research funded by the U.S. military) that students learn best through a one-on-one relationship with an instructor (i.e., "tutoring"). All people. All things. And the difference between one-on-one and classroom is not trivial—it is two standard deviations.[6] "The average tutored student's achievement is better than 98 percent of classroom students," writes Michael Parmentier, former head of Readiness and Training Policy Programs at the Office of the Secretary of Defense.[7]

Why? Here the answer is less clear. As we have seen, we know relatively little for sure about the details of how people learn. But practically speaking, we do have some thousands of years of experience that show us that some things clearly help. A high frequency of interaction. Having your mistakes corrected instantly. Asking frequent questions and getting immediate answers. Making decisions and seeing their consequences. Doing, in situations that require it. Being forced to reflect on what you are doing, reading, or thinking through probing questions. Marshaling your thoughts in formal form. Practice and repetition. Motivation. Although we can't yet articulate all the mechanisms through which they work, we do know these things help people to learn.

But as soon as we move from one-on-one instruction to classrooms, everything we instinctively know about what makes for good learning goes out the window. The frequency of interaction drops to near zero, as does question asking—the average time between questions for individuals in classrooms has been measured at 10 hours.[8] Immediacy of feedback is practically nonexistent. Decision making becomes intermittent. Reflection? You're on your own. Motivation? Only if you're extraordinarily lucky.

So when we uncover the "real" learning question of most of our educational and learning research, we find it is not really "How do people learn?" but "How do we get people to learn in classes (or other groups)?"

I actually think it might be more accurate (although certainly less elegant) to refer to these classes or groups of students, as "herds," and to today's teaching as "herding." Humans have always found it more cost-effective to deal with herds rather than individuals. According to a recent history of food, much early hunting was really herding—driving the whole pack of buffalo over the cliff to get your meat, rather than using a spear.[9] Everyone knows herding animals (or people) who don't want to be herded isn't always easy—you can see in the well-known commercial about herding cats at www.eds.com/advertising/advertising_tv_catherding.shtml—but it's often more "efficient" than one-on-one. We do it in our schools for many reasons. Yet most of us recognize that, despite the fashionable but mostly meaningless noise we hear about "learning communities" and the fact that interaction with others is sometimes useful for learning, students don't learn as much in herds as they would had they been taught exclusively one-on-one.

Herding introduces all sorts of new variables into the mix that are not there with one-on-one, the most obvious being heterogeneity. All teachers know the rule of thumb that you're always going too slowly for one-third of a class and too quickly for another third. (Though a more accurate version might use half.) With one-on-one, though, a learner's particular mix of prior knowledge and abilities, especially "g," are much less of a factor—the good tutor automatically adapts to the level and questions of the learner and provides challenges that are appropriate. The herded student, of course, must adapt to the teacher.

In fact, our instinctive understanding of the importance for learning of homogeneity on the "g" level is why we have a college admission process which—for all its emphasis on certain kinds of diversity—tries hard to sort learners into relatively well-stratified, if not completely accurate, levels of "g." We don't hear about this much from the schools, except through the code word "exclusive," but any kid will tell you whether he (or she) is or isn't "smart enough to get into Harvard." Some even argue that this sorting process alone, and the stamp it gives, is enough, and nothing further has to be learned (this is the Japanese university system).

But whether the herds are homogeneous or not, much research shows—and, more important, everybody knows from experience— that people learn far less when they are herded. Much, if not most of the actual learning takes place *not* in the lecture hall, but when the students are on their own, studying by themselves. And since they typically are given little guidance on how to learn, students must try to puzzle it out for themselves—underlining? cramming? asking your friends? You decide. Unfortunately tutoring—the one proven learning helper that works better than all the others—is left as the method of "last resort" reserved only for when you're not getting it (read "dumb"). Plus, to get this most effective form of instruction, you might have to spend more money on top of the sky-high tuition you are already shelling out!

Assuming, Denying, and Getting Past the Obvious

This is the *real* opportunity of electronic teaching—bringing the benefits of one-on-one instruction to everyone. But achieving this is very different than just putting stuff out there and saying "go at your own pace." The military has been thinking about this for years and has attempted to develop "intelligent tutors." The approach is the right one.

But what have we "educators" done as we've tried to create our (badly named) "e-Learning"? For the most part we have *not* thought carefully about what learning is—different processes, learner controlled, conscious and unconscious, and involving knowledge, tasks, and beliefs. We have *not* differentiated between the types of learning involved and the best strategies for each, but rather just grabbed any old single "theorette" as a "theoretical" basis for our work. (One group has belatedly inserted a "pedagogy" button on each screen, citing someone's favorite "theorette" to justify their work.)

What we *have* done, unfortunately, is taken all the techniques that we have developed and fine-tuned for herding, such as lectures, demonstrations, and tests, put them onto the computer, and assumed they would work. And perhaps worst of all, we have adopted the most meaningless metric of all—screen time available to be viewed—as the basis for buying and selling "learning."

So I say "e-Nough!" To consistently produce true learning, which is what our "e-Learning" needs to accomplish, we will need to do much more. In addition to providing much more motivation through gameplay (see http://www.marcprensky.com/writing/Prensky%20-%20The%20Motivation%20of%20Gameplay-OTH%2010-1.pdf), we will have to take the tutor, not the teacher, as our instructional paradigm, and incorporate all those things that have been obvious to any good tutor for thousands of years: Start where the learner is, provide motivation, keep the tasks challenging but not out of reach, encourage questions, allow for lots of practice. And, to make it reliable, we will need to build on a better, more highly differentiated understanding of learning, which is still to come.

It will also do us no good to deny the facts, even if we don't particularly like them. For example, experience shows that "drill and practice" works better for some people and things than other methods theoretically designed to provide "understanding" (e.g., "Direct Instruction" versus "Open Schools").[10] Let's accept this, even though we might wish it were otherwise, and provide fun, motivating ways to make it happen.

Nor will it help us to spend a lot of time, money, and effort researching the obvious. For example, here are the three "key findings" in the previously mentioned *How People Learn:*

1. Students come to the classroom with preconceptions about how the world works. If their initial understanding is not engaged, they may fail to grasp new concepts and information that are taught, or they may learn them for purposes of a test but revert to their preconceptions outside a classroom.

Breathes there an educator to whom this is news? If there does, and she is not a sweet, 80-year-old kindergarten teacher, what is he or she doing teaching in the 21st century? This is a good example of our research being oriented toward herding, rather than learning, because in classrooms this is hard to do whereas in one-on-one it is a given. A less obvious, but more interesting finding (mentioned only in passing in the book) is that the same is probably true, perhaps even more, for teachers. "In education, a priori beliefs about the way children ought to learn or about the relative value of different kinds of knowledge seem to have tremendous force in shaping judgments about effectiveness," writes Traub.[11]

2. To develop competence in an area of inquiry, students must (a) have a deep foundation of factual knowledge, (b) understand facts and ideas in the context of a conceptual framework, and (c) organize knowledge in ways that facilitate retrieval and application.

Again, does anyone find this a revelation, justifying years of research? This is nothing more than the authors' beliefs about what constitutes "competence." And once more, what they are ultimately concerned with is "How do we develop this when herding?"

3. A "metacognitive" approach to instruction can help students to take control of their own learning by defining learning goals and monitoring their progress in achieving them.

Here, finally, is something worth thinking about. What this says, in plain English, is that just *thinking* about learning can help. Anyone who later in life is able to teach himself or herself something new has clearly learned this, but many of our students never do. As mentioned before, our students get little formal guidance in this area, and often flounder. It would appear that this type of reflection and understanding is something that can and should be codified and taught, quite possibly separate from any subject matter (some call it "learning to learn"). I'm certain we can build much of this into our e-Teaching. But we won't be able to do this totally effectively until we understand more about the process of learning—especially the things that produce the different kinds of learning reliably—rather than just duplicating the teaching environments where learning sometimes occurs.

How can we increase our understanding of what learning is and how to make it happen? Many are looking to neuroscience, with its growing understanding of the brain and how it works, as a potential source of understanding and way out of our dilemma. Does modern neuroscience provide us with the missing answers to our puzzle? As with everything else associated with learning, there are varying opinions. In my next column I will examine the current learning-oriented findings of neuroscientists to see how much guidance—and consistency—we are getting from them that can aid us in our quest to reliably, effectively, and efficiently produce learning in our students. *[Note: This column was never written, but I still hope to do so. Despite the great number of books on the subject, the understanding of learning that neuroscience research has provided us so far appears to me mostly unclear, incomplete, and, in many cases, wrongly interpreted.]*

Notes

1. For a clear up-to-date explanation of "g," see Linda S. Gottfredson, "The General Intelligence Factor," *Scientific American*, November 1998.
2. www.adherents.com/

3. Stan Davis and Jim Botkin, *The Monster Under the Bed*, Simon & Schuster, 1994, p. 151.

4. James Traub, "Does It Work?" *The New York Times* (Education Life), November 10, 2002.

5. www.edge.org/q2003/q03_pinker.html

6. Bloom, B. S. "The Two Sigma Problem: The Search for Methods of Group Instruction as Effective as One-to-One Tutoring," *Educational Researcher*, 13, 4–16, 1984.

7. Michael Parmentier, Advanced Distributed Learning briefing, Spring 2000.

8. Graesser, A. C., & Person, N. K. (1994). "Question Asking During Tutoring." *American Educational Research Journal*, 31, 104–107.

9. Felipe Hernandez-Armesto, *Near a Thousand Tables: A History of Food*, Free Press, 2002, p. 63

10. James Traub, *op. cit.*

11. *Ibid.*

3

Education as Rocket Science

A new metaphor for what educators do

Published in Educational Technology

I believe our teachers are being blamed unfairly, and far too much, for our educational problems. But there is another group—our students—that is blamed even more. Because I spend a great deal of time with students, I know that while they often have (and cause) problems in our schools, when today's kids truly want to learn something, they nearly all can, and do. (We see the greatest evidence for this in their use of video games.) So I decided that a new view of our students was in order—a far more positive view than the "short attention span" rap that students generally get, a view that would both acknowledge students' potential and include their need for motivation. The metaphor I found is reaffirming, both for students and for teachers as well.

છ છ જી જી

*They [the television networks] are still counting horses,
while the world has moved on to counting locomotives.*

—Andrew Rasiej

The metaphor of locomotives versus horses—i.e., of newly acquired, greatly enhanced power in the world that is not yet fully recognized—is a useful one. In education, we can, and should, I suggest, take the metaphor several steps further.

Although we still do herd our kids into classes, they are not, metaphorically speaking, horses. Nor are they locomotives, which, although more powerful, need to stay on tracks that have been laid for them. Nor are they cars, or other vehicles that must remain on a two-dimensional surface (they have, among other things, all moved to 3D). And they are not even jet airplanes, which, although fast, typically fly through the sky on fixed routes so they won't crash into each other.

No, metaphorically, our kids are rockets. Which makes educators, metaphorically, rocket scientists. (Who knew!)

What makes today's kids rockets, rather than anything else? Certainly, at first blush, it's their speed—they operate faster than any generation that has come before. Although nothing may have changed in the rate kids grow up emotionally, there has been enormous change in what today's kids learn and know at early ages, and, therefore in the rate they grow up intellectually. "Kids getting older younger" is a term long in use at MTV. Although parents and teachers still struggle with old definitions of "age appropriate," the term's meaning has changed so much we can hardly recognize it. Even followers of Piaget, such as Edith Ackermann, suggest it is time for a new look at his categories. And while some bemoan this increased speed and want to slow kids down, speed is clearly the reality of today's life, and especially the life of the young.

But what makes today's kids rockets is not just the increased speed. Like rockets, our kids are headed to far-away destinations, places that often those who launch them can't even see. They have been designed (by their 21st century upbringing, especially by the Internet and the complex games many play) to explore, and find out for themselves what works. Like rockets, they often cannot be controlled at every moment, but are initially aimed, as best we can, in the right direction, with mid-course corrections to be made as necessary. And because both kids and rockets are difficult to repair in flight, they both need to be made as self-sufficient as possible.

As with all rockets, our kids' fuel mix is volatile. Some blow up. Some lose their guidance, or their ability to follow direction. Some go off course or stop functioning unexpectedly. Some are faster, and go farther, than others. But many more hit their mark, and it is the job of the rocket scientists to help them do so.

Perhaps most importantly, today's rockets—and kids—can, potentially, go much further, and do things far beyond what any such voyager could do in the past. With the arrival of widely distributed and easy-to-use digital tools, our kids already accomplish, on a daily basis, things that still seem, for many of us, far-off science fiction. They communicate instantaneously with, and learn from, other kids around the globe—*ePals*, the electronic interchange site for kids, reaches every country and territory. They regularly make videos and post them for the world to see and comment on—*YouTube* now has more video than the U.S. TV networks have created in their entire lifetimes. They organize themselves socially and politically across and throughout the planet—governments have already changed policy because of this. *The Globals* is the name the pollster Zogby gives to our "rocket" kids. *The Galactics* is perhaps even a better name. Most of today's kids realize this, at some level, even though many of the adults in their lives don't.

Educators as Rocket Scientists

What does this imply for those whose job is to educate today's kids— kids who can fly around the globe and beyond, further and faster than we ever thought possible? It tells us that we must conceive of what we educators do in a new metaphorical way—not as teachers, but as rocket scientists, building and sending off the best rockets (i.e., students) we possibly can. This means, for one thing, not filling our rocket students up with the old educational fuel of the past, because that fuel just doesn't make today's kids go. We need new fuel, new designs, new boosters, and new payloads.

How do "real" rocket scientists prepare their charges for success? For one thing, they understand that their rockets will likely encounter many unforeseen events and trials, so they work hard to build into the rockets' "brains" (i.e., their software) enough intelligence to get the job done with the minimum of outside help. They build in to the rockets the ability to self-monitor, to self-assess, and to self-correct as much as possible. They create the ability for their rockets to use whatever devices and instrumentation are available to regularly gather data and then analyze it, even as they are speeding along. They perform rigid quality control—not of what the rockets' brains know—that is updatable on-the-fly—but of what they can do with the information they encounter. And while they may pre-program a target, they know that the target will likely change mid-course, and that there are likely to be other changes during the course of the rocket's life.

A Useful Perspective

Seeing our students in this new way—i.e., as rockets—and ourselves as rocket scientists, is incredibly useful and helpful for educators to do. One key reason is that it encourages educators to set the bar for student achievement extremely high—much higher than we currently do. I have often heard educators say that they were "blown away" by what their students accomplished. We should not be blown away by our students, we should be expecting *even more* from them.

Rockets are high-maintenance, and often do require more of our effort and skills to build and keep up. They are also useless on the ground, so that is not where we should prepare them to stay (many of the skills of the ground, have, in fact, been taken over by machines, and are no longer needed for them).

Exploration or Destruction?

What we want is for our rockets, and our kids, to "boldly go where no one has gone before." Depending on the payload installed in their heads at the beginning of the journey, our kids (like real rockets) can be powerful forces for exploration and change, or potential weapons of destruction. Educators (along with parents) install the payload in the rockets that are our kids. Then they send them off to fly into the future, hoping they have prepared them well for what they will meet. Obviously, it is preferable to make the payloads positive, which is why installing ethical behavior—the ability to figure out the right thing to do and to get it done—should be our number one concern as "rocket scientist educators." Our task is to best configure students' brains so they can constantly learn, create, program, adopt, adapt and relate positively to whatever and whomever they meet (and in whatever way they meet them, which increasingly means through technology).

The most important changes required of educators are not technological, but rather conceptual—thinking of themselves as rocket scientists, working with their living, breathing "rockets" as partners. No one—certainly not me—advocates throwing away the past completely. But unless we start preparing our kids to fly really far and land safely, we won't be doing them much good. If we don't start putting some new and different payloads and fuel into the rockets that are in our charge, they will never get off the ground.

4

Turning On the Lights

"Dis-enlightenment," and the splitting of education at the start of the 21st century

Published in Educational Leadership

Few people enjoy being forced to rehear and relearn what they already think they know. Not that every learner gets it perfectly the first time, but, especially in Western culture, correction and guidance is generally a more satisfying path to mastery than rote memorization. I believe that in an age such as ours, when young people know a whole lot more than they ever did, it is a losing educational strategy to assume our students know little or nothing and that our job is to teach them everything, rather than to just shape and guide what they already know and can find out on their own. This essay underscores some of the drawbacks of the old approach and offers some alternatives for motivating and teaching today's students.

෴ ෴ ෴ ෴

Intellectually, kids used to grow up in the dark.
School was their enlightenment. Today, our kids grow up
in the light. And school, sadly, has become the place that
dis-enlightens them.

—Marc Prensky

For most of history, our kids grew up in the dark.

To a young person right up through the mid-20th century, the world was largely an unknown place. Few traveled. Other than what they observed in their own neighborhood, the world was a blank page to them. Some probably heard tales of adventure, war, or der-ring-do. Parents told stories of just how dangerous "out there" really was. Few read widely. How was a kid to tell what was real? In terms of knowing the world you lived in, as a young kid you were pretty much left in the dark.

Except for school.

They day you were sent off to school was the beginning of your enlightenment—the day your window on the world began to open. As you continued on up the grades, the window continued to open wider, and more and more light shone in. From your teachers you learned wonderful things, things that you now knew—because they came from your teachers—to be true.

Your teachers taught you to read, and as you read, more and more of the world became available to you. Images in the books and arti-facts in the museums and other places you visited broadened your knowledge.

Over time, your teachers taught you to do experiments, to test ideas, and to separate, on your own, fact from fiction. You were shown systems and schema to understand things like history, geogra-phy, mathematics, science, and your own and other cultures. You were exposed to civilization's greatest accomplishments, with expla-nations of why they were considered so, and you heard about the names and deeds of the most famous men and women. You learned to think logically, and to structure your own ideas and thoughts, and write them down for others to read and critique.

From Darkness to Light

The shared goal of all your educators was to fling open the curtains of darkness and expose young people like yourself to the richness and diversity of the world, and to people's creations within it. Not every kid found this interesting, of course, and some left school ear-lier than others. But for a great many students, school was truly empowering. School exposed kids for the first time to a wide variety of useful things they knew nothing about, in ways the students were unable to do on their own for themselves.

In fact, the purpose of school (or at least one of its key purposes) was to lead as many kids as possible out of the intellectual darkness into the intellectual light.

And that is what made being an educator a truly "noble" calling: *"We were the people who showed kids the light!"*

Until Now

There's only one problem with this noble thought today—and it's a big one: *Today's kids grow up in the light!* They are deeply immersed in it long before educators ever see them.

Kids today are connected to the entire world, continuously, 24/7, in real time, through myriad personal devices, both electronic (e.g., TV) and digital (e.g., Internet, cell phones) and their media. In the 21st century, how can we characterize the intellectual environment in which our young people grow up? Certainly not one of perfect understanding of the world—after all, they *are* still kids. But could their intellectual state still be characterized, in any sense, as ignorance and darkness? Hardly.

On the contrary, thanks to technology, kids in developed countries such as the United States now grow up knowing about, or being able to find out about pretty much anything from the past or present that may interest them. Google, Wikipedia, and millions of reference sites all stand at their beck and call.

In developed countries such as the United States, the 21st century kid grows up *surrounded* by light, literally, from the first flash of the camera at the moment of birth. They progress to seeing the world through the glow of the TV tube, the sheen of the silver screen, the interactive animations of the computer screen, the LCD on their cell phone, and the screens on their Gameboy Advances, DS Lites or PSPs. They teach each other to actively participate as often as possible in the world—locally and around the globe—through IMs (instant messages), emails, increasingly free calls, and through online connections, discussions, and creative social and communal activities—activities that range from making and sharing music, to helping slow global warming, to helping stop genocide in Darfur.

Long before they ever get to school, kids have seen, compared with the past, a tremendous amount of the world. All their senses—visual, aural, tactile, even taste and smell—have been, electronically, stimulated by the whole world's pictures, foods, behaviors, and cultures. They've watched wars in far-off countries and explorations of distant planets. They've seen wild animals growing up—up-close and personal. They've simulated racing, flying, running businesses. Many have taught themselves to read through the electronic games they play.

Today's kids live their out-of-school life not in the dark, but in the light.

Which doesn't mean everything they see is beautiful. The world kids experience through their devices and connections is still often a scary place for many of them. Full of war and killing, murders of strangers and suicides of friends, the known world can certainly be frightening, perhaps even more so than when kids were ignorant about it. And, certainly, the world is something kids don't yet fully understand.

But it's no longer a dark, unknown place. Today's school kids are not intellectually empty, but arrive at our schools full of knowledge, thoughts, ideas, and opinions about their world and their universe, even though some of what they know may be incomplete, opinionated, or wrong. "Don't think we don't know what's going on or have opinions," says a high school student.

What We *Could* Do

Given this new, changed state of affairs, what do you suppose a smart educator would do? It seems to me that any savvy educator, left on their own, would acknowledge that today's kids grow up differently, and that the kids are enlightened by all their various connections to the world. And those smart educators would figure out ways to use, build on, and strengthen this strong base of connections and reservoir of knowledge with which our kids come to school. Smart educators would assume and expect that kids can use their connections to the light to find information quickly, to structure it in new ways, and to communicate with peers around the world in a powerful, 21st century learning process. They would assign a new role to the teacher: to no longer be the provider of information, but to instead be the explainer, the context provider, the meaning maker, the evaluator of information the kids find on their own, through their electronic connections to the world.

And you know what? That would still be a noble calling, perhaps even more so than before.

Our Choice Instead

But what have we, instead, chosen to do? Somehow educators have decided that all the "light" that our kids are surrounded by—i.e., their electronic connections to the world—is somehow *detrimental* to their education. So systematically, as our kids enter our school buildings, we make them—force them, in fact—to shut off all their connections to the light. No cell phones (if they have one). No music players. No portable TVs. No game machines. In fact, in school, no electronic connection to the world whatsoever is permitted, unless directed and supervised by a teacher. The moment kids get to school, all the *personal* connections they have to the rest of the world—their sources of light—are rudely and disrespectfully stripped from them.

The current generations of students—terribly empowered, used to doing whatever they want whenever they want (think of them as the TiVo "time shifters"), armed to the teeth with the most powerful, most connected technology the world has ever known—are totally dis-empowered. They are told, typically in no uncertain terms, that in school—the place they come to supposedly learn about the world— they are *not allowed* to use their powerful tools—their cell phones, their computers, the open Internet—the lifelines they have learned to employ so fluently to remain in and thrive in the light of their lives.

Back Into Darkness

So what school actually does—quite cruelly, in fact—is force our kids out of the intellectual light of their real, normal lives, into the darkness of the old-fashioned classroom. And therein lies our true danger and our biggest challenge as educators:

> Despite, in most cases, our best intentions, we are no longer the people who show students the light—their light comes from elsewhere, mostly through their technological connections to the world.
>
> And unless we change rapidly, we educators are in grave danger of becoming the people who lead our students *out* of the light, back into darkness.

Perhaps you think I am exaggerating. Do you think this is all just hyperbole? I suggest you listen to the kids: "Whenever I go to school I have to power down," says one. He's not just talking about his devices—he's talking about his brain. "It's like banging your head against the wall," says another.

What do these kids find in their classrooms that they are *allowed* to use? Basal readers. Cursive handwriting. Old textbooks. Outdated equipment.

Yes, that stuff *used to* bring the light to students. But not in the 21st century! For 21st century students, the classroom is a dark, dark place, compared to what they already know and can find out—and its contents provides no more useful light to them than would a tiny 10-watt flashlight on a sunny beach.

But What About Their Teachers?

Hopefully, whenever a kid goes into a classroom, in front of the room is a smiling, friendly, motivated, competent, energetic, knowledgeable, creative, fully prepared teacher, with the ability to individually focus on every kid in his or her class of 40 (and roster of 200) totally undistracted by any personal problems in his or her own life, giving each of the kids every day exciting, personalized work to do—never busy work—and truly motivating every kid to work hard and learn.

The kids I talk to *do* say their best teachers help them, and make a big difference. But they also say there are not enough of them, and that most of their teachers are not like that.

And this is a big problem. Because our kids need help. Not in finding enlightenment—they already have that—but in finding anything interesting to do during the school day.

Bored. Bored. Bored.

The reality is that our school kids, for the most part, are bored to death. And if you don't believe me, or think that the kids have no right to be bored, just pick an average kid, with an average schedule, and "shadow" him or her for a day—go where they go, sit in on all their classes—and see if *you* can stand it. Recently, at a conference of the heads of California's top independent schools, I asked a bright 10-year-old, whose school is considered one of the very best, how often she is bored in class. "Ninety-nine percent of the time" was her immediate answer—she didn't even have to reflect. Others her age answer similarly. "I'm bored nearly all the time, because the teachers just talk and talk and talk," said a fifth grader. Middle and high school kids, even with the best teachers we have, still say with consistency they're bored 50 to 70 percent of the time.

And it makes perfect sense that this should be the case.

- A kid who's seen lunar landings and rovers working on Mars, has done lots of astronomical research on the Internet, and comes to school all excited about space travel is likely to be told "You want to go to space, learn your math." But the math she is taught is not about space, it's 1,200-year-old algebra and 4,000-year-old Egyptian geometry.

- A kid who has read, seen, and possibly written new parts of Harry Potter (on fan sites) is forced to learn the rules of writing, spelling, and literary analysis not from the science fiction and fantasy they enjoy, but from whatever is in the (old) textbooks and whatever (old) books are in the official curriculum.

- A kid who masters the games Caesar III, Age of Kings, Age of Empires, Civilization IV, and Rise of Nations, and therefore knows a huge amount about world history, is likely told "I don't know what's in those games, but it may not be right. And besides, the history you should care about is what will be on the test."

In an era when each student has been able to customize his or her buddy lists, photos, ring tones, cell phone skins, plans, websites, blogs, MySpace and Facebook accounts, and other things for most of their life, our school instruction is mostly "cookie cutter," "one size fits all," and "tell-test." With 40 kids to a class and 900 kids to a counselor, there is little possibility of finding out each kid's passion and addressing their education from that base. "The cookies on my daughter's computer know more about her interests than her teachers do," says Henry Kelly of the Federation of American Scientists. Thank goodness something knows about them!

In a country where most kids can sit at a computer and follow their own interests by hyperlinking anywhere they want to, our instruction has a standard curriculum and standard test for everyone. Sadly, from the kids' perspective, school in the 21st century has become not the place for enlightenment, but the place for *dis*-enlightenment. School, for the most part, brings our kids not out of the dark into the light, but out of the light into darkness.

And until we can figure out how to turn the lights back on for our kids, we educators—once the noble figures who led kids out of the darkness of ignorance—are fast becoming their jailors, locking kids into the darkness of the classroom.

Bifurcation

When I began a few years ago telling educators, in my talks, that our kids' education is bifurcating, I used to get a bunch of blank stares—until

I realized I had to explain that "bifurcating" meant branching in two directions. (I also discovered that most teachers who didn't know this were afraid—or ashamed—to ask.)

"Bifurcation" is an extremely important concept to understand in 21st century education, because it describes exactly what is happening.

In the United States and other developed countries, our kids' education is quickly splitting into two separate—and very unequal— parts. The part we know best, school, is the education that kids, for the most part, are *forced* to experience (by law, so their parents can work). In exchange, school offers the kids a credential, i.e., a diploma and a set of grades, which helps determine their future education and employment.

But "school," in terms of useful learning, is almost entirely irrelevant to the kids' present and future lives. For one thing, it is almost entirely about the past—what we've learned till this point (or some point a while ago) about math, science, language, and social studies— with occasionally a little bit of current events thrown in when there's time or when something really bad, like Columbine or 9/11, happens.

School is certainly *not* about the future, which the kids tell us is their most pressing concern. If it were, it would be full of classes in programming, multimedia literacy and creation, astronautics, bioethics, genomics, nanotechnology, just to name a few future-oriented subjects. The literature kids read and discussed would be alternative visions of the future, i.e., science fiction and fantasy. Students would be learning and practicing in class future-oriented skills such as collaborating around the world electronically and learning to work and create in distributed teams.

I've even heard some school-based educators justify the focus on the past by saying "we don't even know what tomorrows jobs will be—they haven't been invented yet." Perhaps. But that's one huge cop-out. We do know many, if not all, of tomorrow's needed skills, and they're not—almost without exception—the ones being taught in school. If even 20 percent of our current curriculum is relevant to and important for our kids' future lives, I'd be shocked.

Today's kids very much understand this, and so in school, when they are lectured on about the past, they are bored to tears (or, more precisely, to instant messaging and game playing under the desk). They are bored not only by the curriculum offered, but also by the way it is taught. In an era when our society's most creative people spend all their efforts and energy to compete for these kids' attention (think movies, songs, games), our kids' teachers prepare old-fashioned lesson plans, during which, as the student above said, they mostly "talk and talk and talk." School "covers material." It prepares kids for standardized exams. For a ton of reasons that I'm sure you can all cite (NCLB, standards, parent pressure, etc.) school continues to offer, over and over, an outdated "education" that is almost entirely irrelevant.

"After-School"

And if that were the only education our 21st century kids ever got, it would be a real tragedy. But fortunately it is not, because there is another whole dimension to our kids' education. For lack of a better term, I call it "after-school." After-school education is whatever the kids learn when they are *not* in class or doing their homework, or preparing for or taking tests.

Some after-school learning, such as robotics clubs and competitions, and after-school browsing in computer labs, takes place, in fact, in our school buildings. But after-school goes much further. It encompasses, for example, all the time kids spend at home on the Internet. It includes all their blogging and social networking (e.g., in MySpace or Facebook). After-school includes all the time kids spend sharing messages or pictures on their cell phones and creating many of the hundreds of thousands of videos posted on YouTube. It includes the time kids spend in complex games like Runescape and World of Warcraft, and in online non-game worlds such as Whyville, Club Penguin, and Second Life, which are really huge learning environments. After-school includes game and other computer programming classes that kids either sign up for, or teach themselves. It includes the increasing number of non-curricular summer courses, learning camps, and other learning activities.

Who's Preparing Our Kids

It is their after-school education, and not their school education, that is preparing our kids for their 21st century lives, and they know it. This after-school education is not boring to them, because, among other things, they help design it. It's different for every one of them, and there are no exams, but only clear levels of competence, known and respected by everyone.

Can We Compete?

Can school ever compete with after-school to prepare our kids for the future? It had better learn to, because if our schools provide only darkness, and our kids continue to be trapped there by law, doing nothing they consider worthwhile, school will become little more than jail, and sooner or later the kids will rebel and the protests will begin. Already we can see a lot of similarity between our prisons and many of our schools, with both equipped with guards, metal detectors, and people forced into small rooms to do things they don't want to.

School, which should be fighting to compete, and enlisting the most creative thinkers to engage our kids, instead sets up barriers to anyone who wants to contribute. Practically everyone I know who is not involved in the schools but is doing something interesting in education has considered, and ultimately rejected, doing it in schools. This includes museum educators ("We decided to bypass the schools," says Deborah Johnson, Director of Learning at the Museum of Modern Art in New York), physician educators ("Avoid the schools at all costs," advises Dr. James Rosser, laparoscopic surgery teacher at Beth Israel Hospital, also in New York), and many others. It includes especially anyone trying to create any form of education that requires anything remotely resembling "broadband" for large groups simultaneously—schools don't have it, and do not consider getting it at the top of their lists of needs.

How Do We Turn On the Lights?

So is it possible for school to compete? I think so.

But our only hope of doing it, I am sure, is to pretty quickly figure out ways of turning the lights back on for our kids. What makes this particularly challenging is that we need to do this in ways that will work with our current teacher corps, classroom set-ups, and even testing demands. [Note: Doing this is the subject of my book: Teaching Digital Natives: Partnering for Real Learning, written subsequent to this essay.]

The only conceivable way I see for us to even begin to turn on the lights for our kids during school hours is to do *at least* the following:

- *Understand and respect where today's kids are coming from.* I have written about this at great length on my website www.marc prensky.com (free) and in my books *Digital Game-Based Learning* and *Don't Bother Me Mom—I'm Learning* [and, more recently, *Teaching Digital Natives*]. It's less about teachers' learning to use specific new tools or techniques (such as games, blogs, or search engines) as their being willing to "share the work" with the students by allowing the students to use the tools to find and create, while the teacher retains the explainer, context provider, meaning-maker, and evaluator/coach roles mentioned earlier.

The only way to do *this* is for educators to:

- *Continually talk to their students.* This means devoting a meaningful amount of school time (and after-school time if possible) to real, back-and-forth conversation and dialog between students, parents, teachers, and administrators around how the kids want to be, and should be, taught. In my talks to educators, I try to always invite kids to comment and answer audience questions as models for these dialogs. Participants comment that this is at least as beneficial to them as anything I have to say. The kids are pleasantly surprised as well. "I wouldn't have believed it if I hadn't seen it with my own eyes," said one.
- *Understand where the kids are going, i.e., the future, and help them get there.* "Most of us prefer to walk backward into the future," says Charles Handy, "a posture which may be uncomfortable, but which at least allows us to keep on looking at familiar things as long as we can." Most educators today subscribe to this, and are facing backwards, rather than leading their students into the future. If we continue to let any educator at any level feel they have done their job by "covering the material" and "preparing kids for the test" rather than preparing their kids for the future as best as humans can understand it, then our kids will certainly be the losers.

As all the statistics show, our schools have already lost the "grades on past stuff" war to the rest of the world. Kids are already starting to leave the United States for the best education, rather than come here.

Our schools hopefully still have a shot at winning the "creatively preparing kids for the future" war. But we are in real danger of losing that to after-school.

Typically in society, organizations that can't succeed eventually wither and die. Our schools are not succeeding, and in many ways are already showing signs of morbidity. If, as a society, we continue to choose, for whatever reasons, to keep our schools artificially alive by mandating that our kids spend six or so hours a day there, and if our schools continue to offer kids nothing but darkness, something will eventually have to give.

A possible future history lesson: "The school riots began in 2015, and quickly spread around the country. . . ."

Before that happens, let's figure out how to turn on the lights!

5

Digital Natives, Digital Immigrants

(Parts I and II)

Published in On the Horizon

Part I: A New Way to Look at Ourselves and Our Kids

When I first sat down to write this now widely known essay (it has been translated into several languages, and a professor recently wrote that it was "canonical"), I had no idea what it would become. All I knew was that there was a great deal of intergenerational confusion around the then-emerging digital technology. Parents and teachers around the world were surprised and often dismayed to see that their children and students could often learn and master these new technologies much more easily, and with much less stress, than the adults could.

While Doug Rushkoff had already discussed the idea of "native speakers" of technology, and John Perry Barlow had written that adults often "felt like immigrants" in this land, my essay was the first time that anyone had used the terms "Digital Natives" and "Digital Immigrants" together in print. It would certainly not be the last.

I can remember the conversation in which I came up with the idea of a "digital immigrant accent," analogous to the linguistic accent that many immigrants retain. To me, this was always the metaphor's most humorous—and one of its truest—aspects.

Many emailed me from around the world to express their relief that there were "finally" words to describe this phenomenon they had been feeling and observing. The term "Digital Native," in particular, became part of the educational conversation to the point that some educators, observing that their students didn't know everything about technology, wondered—and still wonder—check the Internet—whether the "Digital Native" is a "myth." Here are my original words so you can judge for yourself.

☃ ☃ ☃ ☃

It is amazing to me how in all the hoopla and debate these days about the decline of education in the United States we ignore the most fundamental of its causes. *Our students have changed radically. Today's students are no longer the people our educational system was designed to teach.*

Today's students have not just changed *incrementally* from those of the past, nor simply changed their slang, clothes, body adornments, or styles, as has happened between generations previously. A really big *discontinuity* has taken place. One might even call it a "singularity"—an event which changes things so fundamentally that there is absolutely no going back. This so-called "singularity" is the arrival and rapid dissemination of digital technology in the last decades of the 20th century.

Today's students—K through college—represent the first generations to grow up with this new technology. They have spent their entire lives surrounded by and using computers, video games, digital music players, video cams, cell phones, and all the other toys and tools of the digital age. Today's average college grads have spent less than 5,000 hours of their lives reading, but over 10,000 hours playing video games (not to mention 20,000 hours watching TV). Computer games, email, the Internet, cell phones, and instant messaging are integral parts of their lives.

It is now clear that as a result of this ubiquitous environment and the sheer volume of their interaction with it, today's students *think and process information fundamentally differently* from their predecessors. These differences go far further and deeper than most educators suspect or realize. "Different kinds of experiences lead to different brain structures," says Dr. Bruce D. Perry of Baylor College of Medicine. As we shall see in Part II, it is very likely that *our students' brains have physically changed*—and are different from ours—as a result of how they grew up. But whether or not this is *literally* true, we can say with certainty that their *thinking patterns* have changed. I will get to *how* they have changed in a minute.

What should we call these "new" students of today? Some refer to them as the N-[for Net]-gen or D-[for digital]-gen. But the most useful designation I have found for them is *Digital Natives*. Our students today are all "native speakers" of the digital language of computers, video games, and the Internet.

So what does that make the rest of us? Those of us who were not born into the digital world but have, at some later point in our lives, become fascinated by and adopted many or most aspects of the new technology are, and always will be compared to them, *Digital Immigrants*.

The importance of the distinction is this: As Digital Immigrants learn—like all immigrants, some better than others—to adapt to their environment, they always retain, to some degree, their "accent," that is, their foot in the past. The "digital immigrant accent" can be seen in such things as turning to the Internet for information second rather than first, or in reading the manual for a program rather than assuming that the program itself will teach us to use it. Today's older folk were "socialized" differently from their kids, and are now in the process of learning a new language. And a language learned later in life, scientists tell us, goes into a different part of the brain.

There are hundreds of examples of the digital immigrant accent. They include printing out your email (or having your secretary print it out for you—an even "thicker" accent); needing to print out a document written on the computer in order to edit it (rather than just editing on the screen); and bringing people physically into your office to see an interesting web site (rather than just sending them the URL). I'm sure you can think of one or two examples of your own without much effort. My own favorite example is the "Did you get my email?" phone call. Those of us who are Digital Immigrants can, and should, laugh at ourselves and our "accent."

But this is not just a joke. It's very serious, because the single biggest problem facing education today is that *our Digital Immigrant instructors, who speak an outdated language (that of the pre-digital age), are struggling to teach a population that speaks an entirely new language.*

This is obvious to the Digital Natives—school often feels pretty much as if we've brought in a population of heavily accented, unintelligible foreigners to lecture them. They often can't understand what the Immigrants are saying. What does "dial" a number mean, anyway?

Lest this perspective appear radical, rather than just descriptive, let me highlight some of the issues. Digital Natives are used to receiving information really fast. They like to parallel process and multitask. They prefer their graphics *before* their text rather than the opposite. They prefer random access (like hypertext). They function best when networked. They thrive on instant gratification and frequent rewards. They prefer games to "serious" work. (Does any of this sound familiar?)

But Digital Immigrants typically have very little appreciation for these new skills that the Natives have acquired and perfected though years of interaction and practice. These skills are almost totally foreign to the Immigrants, who themselves learned—and so choose to teach—slowly, step-by-step, one thing at a time, individually, and above all, seriously. "My students just don't _____ like they used to," Digital Immigrant educators grouse. I can't get them to _____ or to _____. They have no appreciation for _____ or _____. (Fill in the blanks, there are a wide variety of choices.)

Digital Immigrants don't believe their students can learn successfully while watching TV or listening to music, because they (the Immigrants) can't. Of course not—they didn't practice this skill constantly for all of their formative years. Digital Immigrants think learning can't (or shouldn't) be fun. Why should they—they didn't spend their formative years learning with *Sesame Street.*

Unfortunately for our Digital Immigrant teachers, the people sitting in their classes grew up on the "twitch speed" of video games and MTV. They are used to the instantaneity of hypertext, downloaded music, phones in their pockets, a library on their laptops, beamed messages, and instant messaging. They've been networked most or all of their lives. They have little patience for lectures, step-by-step logic, and "tell-test" instruction.

Digital Immigrant teachers assume that learners are the same as they have always been, and that the same methods that worked for the teachers when they were students will work for their students now. *But that assumption is no longer valid.* Today's learners are *different.* "Www.hungry.com" said a kindergarten student recently at lunchtime. "Every time I go to school I have to power down," complains a high-school student. Is it that Digital Natives *can't* pay attention, or that they *choose not to?* Often from the Natives' point of view their Digital Immigrant instructors make their education *not worth* paying attention to compared to everything else they experience—and then they blame them for not paying attention!

And, more and more, they won't take it. "I went to a highly ranked college where all the professors came from MIT," says a former student. "But all they did was read from their textbooks. I quit." In the giddy Internet bubble of only a few months ago—when jobs were plentiful, especially in the areas where school offered little help—this was a real possibility. But the dot-com dropouts are now returning to school. They will have to confront once again the Immigrant/Native divide, and have even more trouble given their recent experiences. And that will make it even harder to teach them—and all the Digital Natives already in the system—in the traditional fashion.

So what should happen? Should the Digital Native students learn the old ways, or should their Digital Immigrant educators learn the new? Unfortunately, no matter how much the Immigrants may wish it, it is highly unlikely the Digital Natives will go backwards. In the first place, it may be impossible—their brains may already be different. It also flies in the face of everything we know about cultural migration. Kids born into any new culture learn the new language easily, and forcefully resist using the old. Smart adult immigrants *accept* that they don't know about their new world and take advantage of their kids to help them learn and integrate. Not-so-smart (or not-so-flexible) immigrants spend most of their time grousing about how good things were in the "old country."

So unless we want to just forget about educating Digital Natives until they grow up and do it themselves, we had better confront this issue. And in so doing we need to reconsider both our methodology and our content.

First, our methodology. Today's teachers have to learn to communicate in the language and style of their students. This *doesn't* mean changing the meaning of what is important, or of good thinking skills. But it *does* mean going faster, less step-by step, more in parallel, with more random access, among other things. Educators might ask "But how do we teach logic in this fashion?" While it's not immediately clear, we do need to figure it out.

Second, our content. It seems to me that after the digital "singularity" there are now *two kinds* of content: "Legacy" content (to borrow the computer term for old systems) and "Future" content.

"Legacy" content includes reading, writing, arithmetic, logical thinking, understanding the writings and ideas of the past, etc.—all of our "traditional" curriculum. It is of course still important, but it is from a different era. Some of it (such as logical thinking) will continue to be important, but some (perhaps like Euclidean geometry) will become less so, as did Latin and Greek.

"Future" content is to a large extent, not surprisingly, digital and technological. But while it includes software, hardware, robotics, nanotechnology, genomics, etc., *it also includes the ethics, politics, sociology, languages, and other things that go with them.* This "Future" content is extremely interesting to today's students. But how many Digital Immigrants are prepared to teach it? Someone once suggested to me that kids should only be allowed to use computers in school that they have built themselves. It's a brilliant idea that is very doable from the point of view of the students' capabilities. But who could teach it?

As educators, we need to be thinking about how to teach *both* Legacy and Future content in the language of the Digital Natives. The first involves a major translation and change of methodology; the second involves all that PLUS new content and thinking. It's not actually clear to me which is harder—"learning new stuff" or "learning new ways to do old stuff." I suspect it's the latter.

So we have to invent, but not necessarily from scratch. Adapting materials to the language of Digital Natives has already been done successfully. My own preference for teaching Digital Natives is to invent computer games to do the job, even for the most serious content. After all, it's an idiom with which most of them are totally familiar.

Not long ago a group of professors showed up at my company with new computer-aided design (CAD) software they had developed for mechanical engineers. Their creation was so much better that what people were currently using that they had assumed the entire engineering world would quickly adopt it. But instead they encountered a lot of resistance, due in large part to the product's extremely steep learning curve—the software contained hundreds of new buttons, options, and approaches to master.

Their marketers, however, had a brilliant idea. Observing that the users of CAD software were almost exclusively male engineers between 20 and 30, they said "Why not make the learning into a video game!" So we invented and created for them a computer game in the "first person shooter" style of the consumer games Doom and Quake, called The Monkey Wrench Conspiracy. Its player becomes an intergalactic secret agent who has to save a space station from an attack by the evil Dr. Monkey Wrench. The only way to defeat him is to use the CAD software, which the learner must employ to build tools, fix weapons, and defeat booby traps. There is one hour of game time, plus 30 "tasks," which can take from 15 minutes to several hours depending on one's experience level.

Monkey Wrench has been phenomenally successful in getting young people interested in learning the software. It is widely used by engineering students around the world, with over 1 million copies of the game in print in several languages. But while the game was easy for my Digital Native staff to invent, creating the content turned out to be more difficult for the professors, who were used to teaching courses that started with "Lesson 1—the Interface." We asked them instead to create a series of graded tasks into which the skills to be learned were embedded. The professors had made 5 to 10 minute movies to illustrate key concepts; we asked them to cut them to under 30 seconds. The professors insisted that the learners to do all the tasks in order; we asked them to allow random access. They wanted a slow academic pace, we wanted speed and urgency (we hired a Hollywood script writer to provide this). They wanted written instructions; we wanted computer movies. They wanted the traditional pedagogical language of "learning objectives," "mastery," etc. (e.g., "in this exercise you will learn . . ."); our goal was to completely eliminate any language that even *smacked* of education.

In the end the professors and their staff came through brilliantly, but because of the large mind-shift required it took them twice as long as we had expected. As they saw the approach working, though, the new "Digital Native" methodology became their model for more and more teaching—both in and out of games—and their development speed increased dramatically.

Similar rethinking needs to be applied to all subjects at all levels. Although most attempts at "edutainment" to date have essentially failed from both the education and entertainment perspective, we can—and will, I predict—do much better.

In math, for example, the debate must no longer be about *whether* to use calculators and computers—they are a part of the Digital Natives' world—but rather *how* to use them to instill the things that are useful to have internalized, from key skills and concepts to the multiplication tables. We should be focusing on "future math"—approximation, statistics, binary thinking.

In geography—which is all but ignored these days—there is no reason that a generation that can memorize over 100 Pokémon characters with all their characteristics, history, and evolution can't learn the names, populations, capitals, and relationships of all the 191 nations in the world. It just depends on how it is presented.

We need to invent Digital Native methodologies for *all* subjects, at *all* levels, using our students to guide us. The process has already begun—I know college professors inventing games for teaching subjects ranging from math to engineering to the Spanish Inquisition. We need to find ways of publicizing and spreading their successes.

A frequent objection I hear from Digital Immigrant educators is "this approach is great for *facts,* but it wouldn't work for 'my subject.'" Nonsense. This is just rationalization and lack of imagination. In my talks I now include "thought experiments" where I invite professors and teachers to suggest a subject or topic, and I attempt—on the spot—to invent a game or other Digital Native method for learning it. *Classical philosophy?* Create a game in which the philosophers debate and the learners have to pick out what each would say. *The Holocaust?* Create a simulation where students role-play the meeting at Wannsee, or one where they can experience the *true* horror of the camps, as opposed to the films like *Schindler's List.* It's just dumb (and lazy) of educators—not to mention ineffective—to presume that (despite their traditions) the Digital Immigrant way is the *only* way to teach, and that the Digital Natives' "language" is not as capable as their own of encompassing any and every idea.

So if Digital Immigrant educators *really* want to reach Digital Natives—i.e., all their students—they will have to change. It's high time for them to stop their grousing, and as the Nike motto of the Digital Native generation says, "Just do it!" They *will* succeed in the long run—and their successes will come that much sooner if their administrators support them.

ଔ ଔ ଓ ଓ

Part II: Do They Really *Think* Differently?

The second part of this essay was intended to provide some theoretical background for my previously expressed views. Many debated this part; some, seemingly, never found it. A single typo—the name of the researcher quoted at the start of the article, now corrected here and online—was the cause for a nasty Internet screed, filled with yellow highlighting (apparently to show that its writer's words were not strong enough on their own to combat my ideas ☺).

The issue of whether young people's "brains are changing" is one that has engendered many debates, unfortunately, most of them meaningless. Brain plasticity, at a neuronal level, is now clear and incontrovertible. But the implications of that plasticity are often misunderstood. Exactly what did people think changed, in the past, when we learned something—our butts? We didn't know how brains changed (we are just learning) but we always knew changes took place, because we could observe changes in behavior. (This is, in fact, my definition of learning, in the essay "On Learning" in this volume.)

We certainly know now—if not then—that changes occur in the brain with experience, and, if we define thinking as conscious (at the least) brain activity, we know that "thinking" changes too. But the big question remains "So what?" We are looking, really, for changes on the behavioral level that may be due to different activities and influences. If we in fact could be certain that particular physical brain changes caused particular behavioral changes, and if we had the power to control or even reverse those, that would be one thing. But we aren't sure and don't have that power (yet). Also, if we knew that such changes in structure and behavior were inherited, that would be important, but we don't know that for sure either.

So we are still left with observing the influences and the behaviors, and find-ing the best ways, as educators, to deal with them. We all are aware that today's influences and behaviors are different, in many respects, from those of the past. What follows are my now-10-year-old thoughts on what that might mean.

There is one observation I made in this essay where my thinking has changed substantially over the decade since I wrote it, and that is around the concept of "reflection." At the time, I was offered—and accepted—peoples' opinions that "the ability to reflect" was a big thing being "lost" to this generation. But I now believe quite differently. It is true that slow, verbalized reflection—the kind that teachers see, measure, and encourage, may be less frequent. It may even be true that it comes less easily than before (although I doubt this, because the military has had much success with its "after action reviews," regularly held group reflections on what just happened and why).

What I have learned though—by observing more than anything else—is that reflection does not require, as many claim, "slow" thinking, verbal articulation, or even, often, much, if any, dedicated "time to think." Whenever an intelligent person finishes something and starts it again, hop-ing to improve—be it a round of golf or a video game—their mind quickly and automatically reviews all their mistakes and creates strategies for doing things differently. And this typically happens in bursts that take only small fractions of a second. It is the collection of these "bursts" over time that many refer to as "slow" thinking.

But I do believe that there has to be an incentive for these bursts to hap-pen—some goal the person wants to reach. That is why I believe that if our teachers can discover learning goals that students will adopt as their own (typically tied to students' own passions and interests), reflection will con-tinue to happen, and likely to a degree and in ways that many currently don't think possible.

ଔ ଔ ฏ ฏ

Different kinds of experiences lead to different brain structures.

—Dr. Bruce D. Perry, Baylor College of Medicine

Our children today are being socialized in a way that is vastly different from their parents. The numbers are overwhelming: over 10,000 hours playing video games, over 200,000 emails and instant messages sent and received; over 10,000 hours talking on digital cell phones; over 20,000 hours watching TV (a high percentage fast-speed MTV), over 500,000 commercials seen—all before the kids leave college. And, maybe, *at the very most,* 5,000 hours of book reading. These are today's "Digital Native" students.[1]

In Digital Natives, Digital Immigrants: Part I, I discussed how the differences between our Digital Native students and their Digital Immigrant teachers lie at the root of a great many of today's educational problems. I suggested that Digital Natives' brains are likely *physically different* as a result of the digital input they received growing up. And I submitted that learning via digital games is one good way to reach Digital Natives in their "native language."

Here I present evidence for why I think this is so. It comes from neurobiology, social psychology, and from studies done on children using games for learning.

Neuroplasticity

Although the vast majority of today's educators and teachers grew up with the understanding that the human brain doesn't physically change based on stimulation it receives from the outside—especially after the age of 3—it turns out that that view is, in fact, *incorrect.*

Based on the latest research in neurobiology, there is no longer any question that stimulation of various kinds actually changes brain structures and affects the way people think, and that these transformations go on *throughout life.* The brain is, to an extent not at all understood or believed to be when Baby Boomers were growing up, *massively plastic.* It can be, and is, constantly reorganized. (Although the popular term *rewired* is somewhat misleading, the overall idea is right—the brain changes and organizes itself differently based on the inputs it receives.) The old idea that we have a fixed number of brain cells that die off one by one has been replaced by research showing that our supply of brain cells is replenished constantly.[2] The brain *constantly* reorganizes itself all our child and adult lives, a phenomenon technically known as *neuroplasticity.*

One of the earliest pioneers in this field of neurological research found that rats in "enriched" environments showed brain changes compared with those in "impoverished" environments after as little as two weeks. Sensory areas of their brains were thicker, other layers heavier. Changes showed consistent overall growth, leading to the conclusion that *the brain maintains its plasticity for life.*[3]

Other experiments leading to similar conclusions include the following:

- Ferrets' brains were physically rewired, with inputs from the eyes switched to where the hearing nerves went and vice versa. Their brains changed to accommodate the new inputs.[4]
- Imaging experiments have shown that when blind people learn Braille, "visual" areas of their brains lit up. Similarly, deaf people use their auditory cortex to read signs.[5]
- Scans of brains of people who tapped their fingers in a complicated sequence that they had practiced for weeks showed a larger area of motor cortex becoming activated then when they performed sequences they hadn't practiced.[6]
- Japanese subjects were able to learn to "reprogram" their circuitry for distinguishing "ra" from "la," a skill they "forget" soon after birth because their language doesn't require it.[7]
- Researchers found that an additional language learned later in life goes into a different place in the brain than the language or languages learned as children.[8]
- Intensive reading instruction experiments with students aged 10 and up appeared to create lasting chemical changes in key areas of the subjects' brains.[9]
- A comparison of musicians' versus nonplayers' brains via magnetic resonance imaging showed a 5 percent greater volume in the musicians' cerebellums, ascribed to adaptations in the brain's structure resulting from intensive musical training and practice.[10]

We are only at the very beginning of understanding and applying brain plasticity research. The goal of many who are—such as the company Scientific Learning—is "neuroscience-based education."[11]

Malleability

Social psychology also provides strong evidence that one's thinking patterns change depending on one's experiences. Until very recently Western philosophers and psychologists took it for granted that the same basic processes underlie all human thought. While cultural differences might dictate what people think *about*, the *strategies* and *processes* of thought, which include logical reasoning and a desire to understand situations and events in linear terms of cause and effect, were assumed to be the same for everyone. However this, too, appears to be wrong.

Research by social psychologists[12] shows that people who grow up in different cultures do not just think about different things, they actually *think differently*. The environment and culture in which people are raised affects and even determines many of their thought processes.

"We used to think that everybody uses categories in the same way, that logic plays the same kind of role for everyone in the understanding of everyday life, that memory, perception, rule application and so on are the same," says one. "But we're now arguing that cognitive processes themselves are just far more malleable than mainstream psychology assumed."[13]

We now know that brains that undergo different developmental experiences develop differently, and that people who undergo different inputs from the culture that surrounds them think differently. And while we haven't yet directly observed Digital Natives' brains to see whether they are physically different (such as musicians' appear to be) the indirect evidence for this is extremely strong.

However, brains and thinking patterns do not just change overnight. A key finding of brain plasticity research is that brains do *not* reorganize casually, easily, or arbitrarily. "Brain reorganization takes place only when the animal pays attention to the sensory input and to the task."[14] "It requires very hard work."[15] Biofeedback requires upwards of 50 sessions to produce results.[16] Scientific Learning's Fast ForWard program requires students to spend 100 minutes a day, 5 days a week, for 5 to 10 weeks to create desired changes, because "it takes sharply focused attention to rewire a brain."[17]

Several hours a day, 5 days a week, sharply focused attention—does that remind you of anything? Oh, yes—video games! That is exactly what kids have been doing ever since Pong arrived in 1974. They have been adjusting or programming their brains to the speed, interactivity, and other factors in the games, much as Boomers' brains were programmed to accommodate television, and literate man's brains were reprogrammed to deal with the invention of written language and reading (where the brain had to be retrained to deal with things in a highly linear way).[18] "Reading does not just happen, it is a terrible struggle."[19] "Reading [has] a different neurology to it than the things that are built into our brain, like spoken language."[20] One of the main focuses of schools for the hundreds of years since reading became a mass phenomenon has been retraining our speech-oriented brains to be able to read. Again, the training involves several hours a day, 5 days a week, and sharply focused attention.

Of course, just when we'd figured out (more or less) how to retrain brains for reading, they were retrained again by television. And now things have changed *yet again*, and our children are furiously retraining their brains in even newer ways, many of which are antithetical to our older ways of thinking.

Children raised with the computer "think differently from the rest of us. They develop hypertext minds. They leap around. It's as though their cognitive structures were parallel, not sequential."[21] "Linear thought processes that dominate educational systems now can actually retard learning for brains developed through game and Web-surfing processes on the computer."[22]

Some have surmised that teenagers use different parts of their brain and think in different ways than adults when at the computer.[23] We now know that it goes even further—their brains are almost certainly *physiologically different*. But these differences, most observers agree, are less a matter of kind than a difference of degree. For example as a result of repeated experiences, particular brain areas are larger and more highly developed, and others are less so.

For example, thinking skills enhanced by repeated exposure to computer games and other digital media include reading visual images as representations of three-dimensional space (representational competence), multidimensional visual-spatial skills, mental maps, "mental paper folding" (i.e., picturing the results of various origami-like folds in your mind without actually doing them), "inductive discovery" (i.e., making observations, formulating hypotheses, and figuring out the rules governing the behavior of a dynamic representation), "attentional deployment" (such as monitoring multiple locations simultaneously), and responding faster to expected and unexpected stimuli.[24]

While these individual cognitive skills may not be new, the particular combination and intensity is. We now have a new generation with a very different blend of cognitive skills than its predecessors—the Digital Natives.

What About Attention Spans?

We hear teachers complain so often about the Digital Natives' attention spans that the phrase "the attention span of a gnat" has become a cliché. But is it really true?

"Sure they have short attention spans—for the old ways of learning," says a professor.[25] Their attention spans are *not* short for games, for example, or for anything else that actually interests them. As a result of their experiences Digital Natives crave *interactivity*—an immediate response to their each and every action. Traditional schooling provides very little of this compared to the rest of their world (one study showed that students in class get to ask a question every *10 hours*).[26] So it generally isn't that Digital Natives *can't* pay attention, it's that they *choose not to.*

Research done for *Sesame Street* reveals that children do not actually watch television continuously, but "in bursts." They tune in just enough to get the gist and be sure it makes sense. In one key experiment, half the children were shown the program in a room filled with toys. As expected, the group with toys was distracted and watched the show only about 47 percent of the time as opposed to 87 percent in the group without toys. But when the children were tested for how much of the show they remembered and understood, the scores were exactly the same. "We were led to the conclusion that the 5-year-olds in the toys group were attending quite strategically, distributing their attention between toy play and viewing so that they looked at what was for them the most informative part of the program. The strategy was so effective that the children could gain no more from increased attention."[27]

What Have We Lost?

Still, we often hear from teachers about increasing problems their students have with reading and thinking. What about this? Has anything been *lost* in the Digital Natives' "reprogramming" process?

One key area that appears to have been affected is *reflection*. Reflection is what enables us, according to many theorists, to generalize, as we create "mental models" from our experience. It is, in many ways, the *process* of "learning from experience." In our twitch-speed world, there is less and less time and opportunity for reflection, and this development concerns many people. One of the most interesting challenges and opportunities in teaching Digital Natives is to figure out and invent ways to *include* reflection and critical thinking in the learning (either built into the instruction or through a process of instructor-led debriefing) *but still do it in the Digital Native language.* We can and must do more in this area.

Digital Natives accustomed to the twitch-speed, multitasking, random-access, graphics-first, active, connected, fun, fantasy, quick-payoff world of their video games, MTV, and Internet are *bored* by most of today's education, well-meaning as it may be. But worse, the many skills that new technologies *have* actually enhanced (e.g., parallel processing, graphics awareness, and random access)—which have profound implications for their learning—are almost totally ignored by educators.

The cognitive differences of the Digital Natives *cry out* for new approaches to education with a better "fit." And, interestingly enough, it turns out that one of the few structures capable of meeting the Digital Natives' changing learning needs and requirements is the very video and computer games they so enjoy. This is why "digital game-based learning" is beginning to emerge and thrive.

But Does It Work?

Of course many criticize today's learning games, and there is much to criticize. But if some of these games don't produce learning it is *not* because they are games, or because the concept of "game-based learning" is faulty. It's because *those particular games are badly designed.* There is a great deal of evidence that children's learning games that *are* well designed *do* produce learning, and lots of it—by and while engaging kids.

While some educators refer to games as "sugar coating," giving that a strongly negative connotation—and often a sneer—it is a big help to the Digital Natives. After all, this is a medium they are very familiar with and really enjoy.

Elementary school, when you strip out the recesses and the lunch and the in-between times, actually consists of about three hours of instruction time in a typical 9 to 3 day.[28] So assuming, for example, that learning games were only 50 percent educational, if you could get kids to play them for six hours over a weekend, you'd effectively add a day a week to their schooling! Six hours is far less than a Digital Native would typically spend over a weekend watching TV and playing video games. The trick, though, is to make the learning games compelling enough to actually be used in their place. They must be *real* games, not just drill with eye-candy, combined creatively with *real* content.

The numbers back this up. The Lightspan Partnership, which created PlayStation games for curricular reinforcement, conducted studies in over 400 individual school districts and a "meta-analysis" as well. Their findings were increases in vocabulary and language arts of 24 and 25 percent respectively over the control groups, while the math problem solving and math procedures and algorithms scores were 51 and 30 percent higher.[29]

Click Health, which makes games to help kids self-manage their health issues, did clinical trials funded by the National Institutes of Health. They found, in the case of diabetes, that kids playing their games (as compared to a control group playing a pinball game) showed measurable gains in self-efficacy, communication with parents, and diabetes self-care. And more important, urgent doctor visits for diabetes-related problems declined 77 percent in the treatment group.[30]

Scientific Learning's Fast ForWard game-based program for retraining kids with reading problems conducted National Field Trials using 60 independent professionals at 35 sites across the United States and Canada. Using standardized tests, each of the 35 sites reported conclusive validation of the program's effectiveness, with 90 percent of the children achieving significant gains in one or more tested areas.[31]

Again and again it's the same simple story. Practice—time spent on learning—*works*. Kids don't like to practice. Games capture their attention and make it happen. And of course they must be practicing the right things, so *design* is important.

The U.S. military, which has a quarter of a million 18-year-olds to educate every year, is a big believer in learning games as a way to reach their Digital Natives. They know their volunteers expect this: "If we don't do things that way, they're not going to want to be in our environment."[32]

What's more, they've observed it working operationally in the field. "We've seen it time and time again in flying airplanes, in our mission simulators." Practical-minded Department of Defense trainers are perplexed by educators who say "We don't know that educational technology works—we need to do some more studies." "We KNOW the technology works," they retort. "We just want to get on with using it."[33]

So, today's neurobiologists and social psychologists agree that brains can and do change with new input. And today's educators with the most crucial learning missions—teaching the handicapped and the military—are already using custom designed computer and video games as an effective way of reaching Digital Natives. But the bulk of today's tradition-bound educational establishment seem in no hurry to follow their lead.

Yet these educators know *something* is wrong, because they are not reaching their Digital Native students as well as they reached students in the past. So they face an important choice.

On the one hand, they can choose to ignore their eyes, ears, and intuition, pretend the Digital Native/Digital Immigrant issue does not exist, and continue to use their suddenly-much-less-effective traditional methods until they retire and the Digital Natives take over.

Or they can chose instead to *accept* the fact that they have become Immigrants into a new digital world, and to look to their own creativity, their Digital Native students, their sympathetic administrators, and other sources to help them communicate their still-valuable knowledge and wisdom in that world's new language.

The route they ultimately choose—and the education of their Digital Native students—depends very much on us.

Notes

1. These numbers are intended purely as "order of magnitude" approximations; they obviously vary widely for individuals. They were arrived at in the following ways. (Note: I am very interested in any additional data anyone has on this.)

Video games: Average play time: 1.5 hours/day (Source: "Interactive Videogames," *Mediascope,* June 1996). It is likely to be higher five years later, so $1.8 \times 365 \times 15$ years = 9,855 hours.

Emails and instant messages: Average 40 per day $\times 365 \times 15$ years $= 219, 000$. This is not unrealistic even for pre-teens—in just one instant messaging connection there may be over 100 exchanges per day—and most people do multiple connections.

TV: "Television in the Home, 1998: Third Annual Survey of Parent and Children," Annenburg Policy Center, June 22, 1998, gives the number of TV hours watched per day as 2.55. M. Chen, in the *Smart Parents Guide to Kid's TV* (1994), gives the number as 4 hours/day. Taking the average, 3.3 hours/day $\times 365$ days $\times 18$ years = 21,681.

Commercials: There are roughly 18 30-second commercials during a TV hour. 18 commercials/hour $\times 3.3$ hours/day $\times 365$ days $\times 20$ years (infants *love* commercials) = 433,620.

Reading: Eric Leuliette, a voracious (and meticulous) reader who has listed online every book he has ever read (www.csr.utexas.edu/personal/leuliette/fw_table_home.html), read about 1,300 books through college. If we take 1,300 books $\times 200$ pages per book $\times 400$ words per page, we get 104,000,000 words. Read at 400 words per minute gives 260,000 minutes, or 4,333 hours. This represents a little over 3 hours/book. Although others may read more slowly, most have read far fewer books than Leuliette.

2. Paul Perry in *American Way,* May 15, 2000.

3. Renate Numella Caine and Geoffrey Caine, *Making Connections: Teaching and the Human Brain,* Addison-Wesley, 1991, p. 31.

4. Dr. Mriganka Sur, *Nature,* April 20, 2000.

5. Sandra Blakeslee, *New York Times,* April 24, 2000.

6. Leslie Ungerlieder, National Institutes of Health.

7. James McLelland, University of Pittsburgh.

8. Cited in *Inferential Focus Briefing*, September 30, 1997.

9. Virginia Berninger, University of Washington, *American Journal of Neuroradiology*, May 2000.

10. Dr. Mark Jude Tramano of Harvard. Reported in *USA Today*, December 10, 1998.

11. *Newsweek*, January 1, 2000.

12. They include Alexandr Romanovich Luria (1902–1977), Soviet pioneer in neuropsychology, author of *The Human Brain and Psychological Processes* (1963), and, more recently, Dr. Richard Nisbett of the University of Michigan.

13. Quoted in Erica Goode, "How Culture Molds Habits of Thought," *New York Times*, August 8, 2000.

14. John T. Bruer, *The Myth of the First Three Years*, Free Press, 1999, p. 155.

15. G. Ried Lyon, a neuropsychologist who directs reading research funded by the National Institutes of Health, quoted in Frank D. Roylance "Intensive Teaching Changes Brain," *SunSpot*, Maryland's Online Community, May 27, 2000.

16. Alan T. Pope, research psychologist, Human Engineering Methods, NASA. Private communication.

17. *Time*, July 5, 1999.

18. *The Economist*, December 6, 1997.

19. Kathleen Baynes, neurology researcher, University of California—Davis, quoted in Robert Lee Hotz, "In Art of Language, the Brain Matters," *Los Angeles Times*, October 18, 1998.

20. Dr. Michael S. Gazzaniga, neuroscientist at Dartmouth College, quoted in Robert Lee Hotz, "In Art of Language, the Brain Matters," *Los Angeles Times*, October 18, 1998.

21. William D. Winn, Director of the Learning Center, Human Interface Technology Laboratory, University of Washington, quoted in Peter Moore, *Inferential Focus Briefing*, September 30, 1997.

22. Peter Moore, *Inferential Focus Briefing*, September 30, 1997.

23. *Ibid.*

24. Patricia Marks Greenfield, *Mind and Media: The Effects of Television, Video Games and Computers*, Harvard University Press, 1984.

25. Dr. Edward Westhead, professor of biochemistry (retired), University of Massachusetts.

26. Graesser, A. C., & Person, N. K. (1994) "Question Asking During Tutoring," *American Educational Research Journal*, 31, 104–107.

27. Elizabeth Lorch, psychologist, Amherst College, quoted in Malcolm Gladwell, *The Tipping Point: How Little Things Can Make a Big Difference*, Little Brown & Company, 2000, p. 101.

28. John Kernan, President, The Lightspan Partnership. Personal communication.

29. "Evaluation of Lightspan. Research Results From 403 Schools and Over 14,580 Students," February 2000, CD ROM.

30. Debra A. Lieberman, "Health Education Video Games for Children and Adolescents: Theory, Design and Research Findings," paper presented

at the annual meeting of the International Communications Association, Jerusalem, 1998.

31. Scientific Learning Corporation, National Field Trial Results (pamphlet). See also Merzenich et al., "Temporal Processing Deficits of language-Learning Impaired Children Ameliorated by Training" and Tallal et al., "Language Comprehension in Language Learning Impaired Children Improved With Acoustically Modified Speech," *Science,* Vol. 271, January 5, 1996, pp. 27–28, 77–84.

32. Michael Parmentier, Director, Office of Readiness and Training, Department of Defense, The Pentagon. Private briefing.

33. Don Johnson, Office of Readiness and Training, Department of Defense, The Pentagon. Private briefing.

6

The Emerging Online Life of the Digital Native

What kids do differently because of technology, and how they do it

An eternal work-in-progress

As I write, there is a great educational debate going on about the use and educational value to students of the so-called "virtual" (i.e., online) world in its many forms. Some educators see it as a boon. Perhaps more see it as a huge threat and danger to students and to education. Many adults rush to remind young people that actions in the virtual world can "cross over" into the nonvirtual world—as if concepts like "separating work and pleasure" or "public and private lives" were a new problem in the world rather than one just made different (and possibly more complicated) by new technology.

Second Life, while perhaps not the best software ever written, is possibly the most aptly named. For that is exactly the new opportunity our kids are being offered: the ability to have second, and often completely separate, lives. The idea of a second life is also not, of course, new to the world, as many adults have one, either by having family in two places or by participating in different, culturally isolated, activities. But up until now, this has not been available to children, except through their imaginations (how many kids have an "imaginary friend," for example?).

Now it is possible for kids to have more than one life—our children (not yet all, but a great many) have access to online lives in addition to the real ones. In some cases these multiple lives intersect, cross over, and impact each other, but not always. And although there sometimes may be negative consequences, there often are not. Today's young people go online to play, learn, find work, date, and even marry happily, in many cases.

There are two big mistakes that I see far too many adults making. One is to see the online lives as "inferior" to the offline ones and the other is to see the online lives as less "real." To young people, both lives are real (if not real world) and both, in different instances, can be equally good, or better. Offline, kids often judge each other by how they look physically. Online, they can only see, and judge by, each other's work product.

Adults, at differing speeds, are beginning to understand these distinctions, and to figure out where each world provides greater advantages. While few, I assume, would want to do all their bathing in the online world, many are happy to do all their research there.

The essay that follows was my attempt to chronicle young people's emerging digital life early on. My original intention was to put this on the Web as a "living document" that I and others would update often, but that didn't happen. So you, the reader, can supply all the updates in your own (real? virtual?) mind.

᎒ᏺ ᎒ᏺ ᏏᎧ ᏏᎧ

One of the most interesting things I enjoy observing about young people today is the rich online worlds and lives they are in the process of creating for themselves.

For almost every activity in their lives, these so-called Digital Natives (see "Digital Natives, Digital Immigrants," at www.marc prensky.com/writing/default.asp [and elsewhere in this volume]) are inventing new, *online* ways of making each activity happen, based on the new technologies available to them.

This is not to say that *every* young person does *every* one of these things online—many still do only a few—but the *possibilities* for what Digital Natives can do online are growing exponentially and are being adapted by more and more of them daily (and by some adults as well, although as we will see, there are differences).

A 2004 survey by the NetDay project of 200,000 U.S. students (www.netday.org) concluded that "students are not just using technology differently today, but are approaching their lives and their daily activities differently because of the technology."

Says one teenage girl in a Yahoo video, "On the Internet you can play games, you can check your mail, you can talk to your friends, you can buy things, and you can look up things that you really like."

And the Internet is just the tip of an enormous iceberg of possibilities. As important as it may be to the Digital Natives, their online lives are a whole lot bigger than just the Internet. This online life has become *an entire strategy for how to live, survive, and thrive in the 21st century,* where cyberspace is a part of everyday life. Today's third graders, as the NetDay study observed, already have multiple email addresses.

In the paragraphs that follow I look at a large number of daily activities that *all* people do—including "Digital Immigrants"—to observe and examine just how the Digital Natives have taught themselves, and learned, to do these activities differently.

One thing we observe is that even when Immigrants use the *exact same* technology, such as eBay, or blogs, Natives and Immigrants typically do things differently. This often causes dissonance and disconnect between the two groups. If you haven't felt this dissonance, at least in some areas, I bet you haven't been with a lot of people from the other age group.

Also, as far as I can observe from the countries I've been to in the past few months, from Scotland to Italy, to New Zealand, to Japan, to Canada, the phenomenon I am describing is global in the developed world and is quickly emerging in other countries as well.

Areas of Change

So, here follow a number of areas in which the Digital Natives are creating their own way of doing things, often "under the radar" of most Digital Immigrant adults. Although this is a relatively long list—which is part of my point—I do some summarizing at the end. (If you are impatient, or hate lists, just skip to the final paragraphs.)

Digital Natives Are **Communicating** Differently *Email, instant messaging, chat*

All human communication changed radically with the advent of the worldwide computer network, and for no group more so than Digital Natives. Letters, which once took time and thought to write and time to arrive, were quickly supplemented and often supplanted by email, which could be written quickly and sent instantly to any number of people. But while Digital Immigrants spent, and still spend time worrying about which type of communication was better, the Digital Natives quickly abandoned any pretense of traditional letter writing ("You mean on paper?" asked one incredulously) except when forced to do it by a traditionalist parent or teacher.

At the same time, long-distance communication went from being expensive (and therefore time limited) to being essentially free. This opened up to the Natives the possibility of frequent, worldwide communication, and, again, they have quickly adapted it to their own purposes, just as their parents did in the office. It is now possible for the Natives to remain in close communication with anyone they meet, anywhere, and they often do, expanding and simplifying the traditional notion of "pen pals." While companies like ePals have sprung up to protect kids, most prefer, certainly with people they know, to remain unguided and unfiltered.

Email, and even more its synchronous cousin, chat, allowed another new phenomenon to emerge—online-only acquaintances and friends. Digital Natives began realizing that you could meet people online in various news and discussion groups, and that they would be people who shared your interests. Not only that, but you could read their posts and see how they thought long before you ever contacted them, even online.

Kids quickly realized that "lookism," that seldom-talked-about but insidious social divider, doesn't exist at all on the Web, and they were thrilled to take advantage of this, with the ones who might be the least communicative in person reaping some of the biggest benefits.

(Of course with this comes the dangers of predators and criminals, which are real, but the Natives are not about to let this spoil their party. As we shall see in a minute, they have begun to create and evolve online reputation systems to keep themselves and their friends safe—or at least safer—in the digital world.)

Email is a form of what is called "asynchronous" communication. Asynchronous means that only one of the communicating parties needs to be there at a time; the message is composed and sent at the writer's convenience, and is read at the receivers,' just like "snail mail" (as the Digital Natives have dubbed the post office system). This type of communication has great advantages, including the time to reflect before you write or answer. While the "etiquette" that has evolved for email demands a quick response, that response does not have to come within the hour or even the same day. So, as fast as it is, email is the Native's "reflective" form of communicating.

But this does nothing for those who like their communications to be "synchronous," that is, live and "real time." One form of real-time communication, of course, is the phone, and for Digital Natives the cell phone has become a necessity, as we shall hear more about later. But another form of real-time communication, used by the Natives to a much greater extent than by their elders, is chat, also known, in various incarnations as instant messaging (IM) and real-time texting. Coming in a number of forms or flavors, chat are text-based systems in which typically everyone in the conversation, which can be two people only or very large numbers, is online simultaneously. Today's Digital Natives thrive on this form of communication—every parent I talk to marvels (and even sometimes brags) at the number of "chat windows" their kids have open simultaneously—often not realizing that this is universal. Most of these conversations are one-on-one, but some are in chat rooms, where the various "speakers" are identified by their online names or "handles" before their comments.

Obviously, texting is slower than just talking, so the Digital Natives have invented ways to speed it up. "Correct" spelling is replaced by whatever is readable. Anything that can be done with one key is: "k" for okay, "c" for see, "u" for you (as in "cu later"). Numbers replace their homonyms (as in t42) and the way characters look on the screen takes on meaning. Abbreviations are well known (LOL = laugh out loud). Brief communications like H4T5TNT (home for tea at five tonight) are common and are often made up among particular users. And a semi-secret (but widely known among the Natives) code has evolved to protect texters privacy, as in "GTGPOS" (got to go, parent over shoulder).

I have heard from numerous parents stories about how children who had trouble communicating using normal speaking, writing, or even email (because of some form of dyslexia or shyness, for example) completely blossom in the norm-free communication atmosphere of chat, texting, and IM, where the only "rule" is to make yourself understood.

The "missing" communication elements of facial observation and body language are often approximated in both email and texting by "emoticons" such as the happy, sad, or winking face or the textual equivalent (<grin>), enriching the communication. And while it is harder, perhaps, to tell if someone is lying when you don't see them in person, technology is addressing this too, through voice pattern and biometric analyses.

An important phenomenon is that all the various elements of the Natives' digital life are closely related. Chat, for example, plays a big role in games. Depending on the situation, chat may be preferred to voice communication, even when available, because it is more private.

Advertisers, who watch kids' behaviors carefully, have already picked up on this in their sales pitches, such as the TV commercial in which a group of skiers in a gondola, as a practical joke, silently text message each other to lure one friend out of the car prematurely.

Digital Natives Are **Sharing** Differently *Blogs, webcams, camera phones*

While email and texting are clearly mechanisms for sharing, Digital Natives have evolved other, specific mechanisms to do so. Take blogs, for example (the term *blog* is a shortening of *weblog*). These text-only (originally) sites allow Digital Natives to share the most intimate details of their personal and emotional lives on a weekly, daily, or even hourly basis. Software has been developed that let kids with online access set up a personal blog at almost no cost. (See www.blogster.com.) The entries get archived, and the blogs remain permanently online, accessible to anyone with the address or a link.

Blogs have led to a complete reversal of the "diary" phenomenon—whereas once kids kept their feelings locked up in a book, today they (or at least many of them) prefer to post them online for all to see and share. Friends read each other's blogs to know what's going on in the social group. Important features of blogs are lists of links to other blogs that the writer enjoys, so they serve as a form of interconnection.

The blogging phenomenon, of course, has also entered the Digital Immigrant world, but in a very different way—as an *intellectual* sharing tool. Many intellectuals, from news people to "gurus" to professors, write and publish blogs, which become regular reading for their followers. But because the usage is so different (emotion versus intellect), this is effectively a different medium than the blogs of the Digital Natives.

Cell phone cameras are now the primary means of sharing images among young people, either sending the pictures or passing the cell phone around, as I often see schoolgirls doing on the subway. Photo albums appear to be a thing of the past.

Webcams are another device Digital Natives use frequently for sharing, while Digital Immigrants use them typically for monitoring. As a "sharing" phenomenon, webcamming consists of setting up one or more cheap, tiny video cameras that broadcast continually to a website. Digital Natives might share continuous views of their rooms, something in nature, a pet—often the weirder the better. Immigrants, on the other hand, typically use webcams for "monitoring" in a security or similar situation, such as a "babycam." As a preview of the

Digital Native's future, I recently watched a form of webcam sharing in which a technology-oriented father on the Internet searched the webcams in each room in his house in order to share with me "live" pictures of the baby.

Digital Natives Are **Buying and Selling** Differently *eBay, schoolwork*

Shopping—who would have imagined the extent to which the digital revolution has changed it? While for Immigrants the Internet has brought convenience, comparison, and collectibles, for Natives is has brought access to new wealth and access, mainly through the ability to purchase clothing, computers, and other things on eBay. I know of schoolgirls who buy all their clothes on eBay—and dress only in designer ware. For equipment geeks, the Web, and eBay in particular, are a source of never-ending flea market.

Of course it also didn't take the Natives long to figure out that the Web is a great place to buy and sell school-related information—in particular papers and exams. This has, unfortunately, led their Immigrant professors to become digital sleuths rather than searching for and inventing new teaching methods.

eBay has also become the place for Digital Natives to "monetize," if they choose, the work they do in a game, by offering for sale advanced characters, weapons, and other items. This has led one economics professor to conclude, by assuming that the relative value of the assets sold online was applied to everything in the game, that the online game EverQuest has a larger economy than Russia!

One other important thing that Digital Natives have learned to buy and sell online is their services, as freelancers, employees, and even spouses. The Web is now the preferred means of finding a job (not to mention a mate). And chances are good that your Digital Native son or daughter will be finding some or all of their dates online.

Digital Natives Are **Exchanging** Differently *Music, movies, humor*

Digital Natives love to trade, to give and get, especially items that express their personalities, such as songs, movies, and websites. Sites that are humorous get passed around particularly quickly, in what has now become known as the "viral" way. This has led to a great clash with the old system, as young people increasingly see things available to them online as "free" of ownership and cost. Although legislation and some widely publicized prosecutions have slowed this sharing down somewhat in the United States, I predict this is just temporary as new business models evolve. Although the 99 cent song has made some headway in the United States, free music and video file sharing continues unabated and at record paces around the world and in most of our colleges. The data shows a continual increase of peer-to-peer (P2P) activity, and P2P applications are still the most downloaded on the Internet.

Digital Natives Are **Creating** Differently *Sites, avatars, mods*

One of the defining characteristics of the Digital Native is the desire to create. Digital Natives are adept (or become quickly so, given the chance) at building websites, Flash movies, and other online creations. In their games they create not only avatars (characters to represent them), but entire worlds, including the houses, furniture, clothes, weapons, and implements of whatever world they are inhabiting. More and more games now come with tools, such as "level editors" included in the box, which allow interested players to create entirely new worlds and games of their own invention. This process, known as "modding," has a huge number of participants, who create everything from levels to complete games (total modifications) some of which get sold separately. Prizes of up to $1 million are offered for this (usually collaborative) skill. Mods that use the same tools to create passive movies rather than interactive games are known as "Machinima" and they too have a large creative force and following on the Web (try Googling "machinima"). In many games the volume of player-created content equals or surpasses content created by the game developers.

The important point here is about tools. Digital Natives expect to have powerful tools available to them, and they know, by teaching themselves and teaching each other, how to use them.

Digital Natives Are **Meeting** Differently *3D chat rooms, dating*

Meeting used to be considered purely a face-to-face activity. Obviously, people still do meet face to face, but online meeting and arranging meetings online has become an important hallmark of this generation. All kinds of software exist to facilitate this, from instant messaging "chat rooms" to tools like "wikis" and "Net meeting." There are tools to help people set up live meetings, such as www .meetup.com. In Japan, people use their cell phones as a meeting mechanism, setting profiles in a program called Lovegety, which set both phones ringing when passersby's profiles match up.

Digital Natives Are **Collecting** Differently *mp3, video, sensor data*

I don't know how many Digital Natives still collect stamps, but I do know they collect a lot of songs and videos—the statistics are that 2 *billion* songs are downloaded per month. Young people exchange music as an expression of who they are, and although some are pay-ing for songs under the new schemes from Apple and others, most of what is collected is exchanged and downloaded for free. Peer-to-peer applications that facilitate this collecting are the most downloaded apps on the Net.

Digital Natives Are **Coordinating** Differently *Projects, workgroups, MMORPGs*

Teachers would be jealous if they had any idea to what extent Digital Natives are able to coordinate their activities online and to run projects that may involve hundreds of people. One classic example is that when a game didn't have a wide enough variety of spaceships to suit the players, the players just set up their own teams to create more of them. Some made the wire frame models, others the "skins," others the weapons for these very complex creations, and through a totally ad hoc coordination process they got added to the game.

In massive multiplayer online role playing games, or MMORPGs, such as RuneScape, Toontown, EverQuest, Lineage, Dark Age of Camelot, Star Wars Galaxies, and City of Heroes (to name only some), players form groups, either ad hoc or standing, to work together on tasks such as freeing a building or storming a castle. Some groups are formed quickly as required, but others are long-lasting clans or guilds, where players have had to prove their skill to join and pledge to be available when needed. Imagine 50 to 100 players, all with dif-ferent powers, all going at a certain hour into the online world together (from wherever in the physical world each of them happens to be) to storm a castle—and the castle defenders frantically contact-ing each other to get online to defend. (Actually, you don't have to imagine this at all—an animation of screenshots is online at http:// www.youtube.com/watch?v=mHyubYqczDs.)

Many aspects of these complex forms of self-coordination are sec-ond nature to today's game players and to Digital Natives in general.

Digital Natives Are **Evaluating** Differently *Reputation systems: Epinions, Amazon, Slashdot*

When one is working with other people online—people one may never meet face to face—it is useful and important to have ways to evaluate whether to trust and believe them. While people with little online experience fret a lot about this (and while online predators do exist and kids need to be careful), much has been done in the online world, by Digital Natives and others, to allow people to establish and rely on online reputations.

One of the most widely used ways of establishing a reputation is though rating systems. If you buy or sell on eBay or Amazon, you get to rate the opposing buyer and seller on their promptness, honesty, efficiency, and so on. Bad apples get weeded out and good ones rise to the top. On group blogs such as Slashdot.com (an information site for nerds) and others, people's posts—comments—get rated by the community, from worthless (1) to insightful (5). You the user can set your filter to see only comments of a certain caliber or only comments from people with a certain reputation. While some Immigrants may see all these rating opportunities (rate this page, rate this post) as intrusions, or wastes of time, Natives know their online compass depends upon them and are often more eager to comply.

Of course, at the same time one is evaluating others' behavior and content, one is building up one's own reputation. By being honest, following norms (for example, no cursing or "shouting" by using ALL CAPS when posting), and being thoughtful in comments and posts, one builds up a positive online reputation. Building a negative online rep, or a mixed one, is possible as well.

And as one spends more time online, one's presence and reputation is there for all to see—unlike in the offline world—and can be determined, at one level, by just Googling a person's name. The number of people linking to them (which determines in large part their Google positions) as well as the online work they have created, will speak for itself.

Digital Natives Are **Gaming** Differently *"Versus," small and large groups*

The experiences called "games" by the Digital Natives are totally different than what their Digital Immigrant parents called (and still call) "games," and this difference lies at the root of much of the objection to and rejection of games by teachers, parents, and others. Although there is some holdover—known today as casual or mini-games—games today are not the games of the previous generation. Those games—mostly card, board, and word games—were typically short, uncomplicated, and even trivial (with a big one even named Trivial Pursuit). The old games could be won in a couple of hours at most, often much less.

Today's best-selling computer and video games, by contrast, are deep, complex experiences that take anywhere from 30 to more than 100 hours to finish. And even today's so-called casual and mini-games, which take less time, deliver a much more intricate, adaptive experience than in the past.

Today's games are also almost exclusively multiplayer. Although in many Digital Immigrants' minds computer and video gaming means "one individual in front of a machine," solo gaming is pretty much passé—an artifact of the aberrant time when computers were not yet connected. Gaming with others now has so many components that there is something there for everyone. Games (although not the same games) are played by people of all ages and social groups. Multiplayer games involve anywhere from two players to up to a million players. Recently a female college senior, a software engineering major who is the top student in her class, admitted to me that she has been a "closet" game player for years, not telling anyone outside of her gaming friends for fear of being laughed at, but that now she is ready to "come out."

Digital Natives Are **Learning** Differently *About stuff that interests them*

Digital Native learning is also very different. Of course it only happens in its true form for things the Natives want to learn about (hobbies, vacations, games, for example), but the Natives are very much aware that if they *want* to learn something (usually for their own purposes), the tools online are available for them to do it on their own. Recently when a 12-year-old, whose in-school problems were giving his parents fits, wanted a pet lizard, he spent days searching the Web for everything he could find on different types of lizards as pets, and the advantages and disadvantages of each, and presented his parents with a 20-page report. (He didn't get the lizard, but his parents were impressed, as was I.) A third grade girl became interested in butterflies and, on her own, prepared a report that totally impressed her teacher and her classmates.

Today, when a student is motivated to learn something, she has the tools to go further in her learning than ever before—far beyond her teachers' ability and knowledge, and far beyond what even adults could have done in the past. The Digital Natives exploit this to the fullest, while ignoring, to a larger and larger extent, the things they are *not* motivated to learn, which, unfortunately, includes most, if not all, of their schoolwork.

Digital Natives Are **Searching** Differently *Info, connections, people*

Search is now the second biggest use of the Internet, after email. A great deal of what the Digital Natives do online involves searching—for information, products, people, connections—and the Natives have very sophisticated tools available to them for this purpose.

Did you know you can use Google to search for phone numbers, dictionary definitions, and online images? The Natives do. Build a better search tool, such as Google did when others were using more primitive engines such as Yahoo and Alta Vista, and the Natives will switch en masse overnight. This is why Microsoft has spent $100 million to move into the search business.

Is Native searching different from Immigrant searching? Certainly, in terms of the topics searched. And there are also differences, I think, in the type of information each is looking for. Immigrants, in general, want the most filtering—they get overwhelmed easily by lots of information; Natives prefer more raw information so they can filter for themselves. (I've never heard a Digital Native complain about "information overload"—it's a fact of life for them.)

While teachers often complain about their students' inability to discriminate among good, bad, true, false, useful, or un-useful information, this ability is not lacking in general, but only in the domains the students don't understand well. It is not at all true in domains that they understand—give boys raw information about games or skateboards, or girls information about social groups to which they belong, and they will discriminate just fine.

Digital Natives Are **Analyzing** Differently *SETI, drug molecules*

Digital Natives have volunteered in large numbers (along with many Immigrants, to be sure) to be part of massive analysis projects, by running Internet-connected "screen saver" programs that download chunks of data and use their computer's free processor cycles to analyze them and send back the results.

Data that is being analyzed in this "distributed" way include the information from the SETI (Search for Extraterrestrial Intelligence) project of the University of California, and programs to search through millions of possible drug combinations for the few that seem promising against certain diseases.

Digital Natives are also more open to themselves and especially their devices being sensors, providing data for large projects, such as reporting conditions such as weather simultaneously around the world.

Digital Natives Are **Reporting** Differently *Moblogs, digital photos*

In contrast with their parents, who used to love to keep any information they had secret ("Knowledge is power" was their motto), Digital Natives love to share and report information as soon as they receive it (perhaps "Sharing knowledge is power" is their new, unvoiced, motto). As soon as the Web appeared, Digital Natives began using it as a reporting tool about their lives and their interests. With a free website or a blog, any kid can be an online reporter on any topic. Digital Native websites and blogs exist about every topic, from politics to entertainment. Extreme forms of reporting include the stories of many kids who went to see the movie *The Hulk,* expecting it to be a big blockbuster, text messaging their friends from the theater that the movie was a dud before the movie had even ended.

Digital cameras and video cams, and particularly cell phone cameras and webcams, let Natives report in completely new ways. Moblogging (mobile blogging), for example is the phenomenon by which people enter data into their blog (via pictures, voice, or texting) from their cell phones while on the go.

Digital Natives Are **Programming** Differently *Open systems, mods, search*

Pretty much every Digital Native can program to some extent, even if it is only setting up and personalizing his or her cell phone or using "and" or "or" in search engines. Many, or course, program to a far greater extent, even those who have not studied programming formally (though today more and more have). Today, in fact, we have a situation similar to ancient times when only a few people (known as "scribes") could read and write. If you needed to send a letter, you went to a scribe, who created it for you. Today, if you need a program to do something, such as, for example, collecting political contributions online, you would go to a Digital Native programmer, who would create whatever you need, from a website to a program, often in a matter of hours.

In addition, programming is spreading quickly among Digital Natives in the form of graphical programming languages, particularly Macromedia's Flash. Many young people can program successfully in this language, and banks of free code modules are quickly being established to make it even easier. (A great example was the *This Land Is Your Land* clip that drew national attention during the 2008 U.S. presidential election, but that is just one noninteractive example of the many things Flash is capable of. All kinds of expressions and games are emerging—see www.socialimpactgames.com for lots of examples.) In a short time Flash players will be incorporated into all new cell phones, so that Natives can share their programming on phones as well as on the Web.

Digital Natives Are **Socializing** Differently *Learning social behavior, influence*

Digital Natives are both socializing online and "being socialized," as the social scientists say. Their online contacts are as "real" to them as their face-to-face ones, albeit different in style. In a positive sense, online relationships are not affected by the "lookism" and status that is so important and frustrating in kids' face-to-face social lives—online, you and other people are judged only by what you say and produce. Reputation and influence are earned and not based on social caste. Yet, as in the face-to-face world, group norms of behavior must be learned and followed, often on pain of ostracism—again, try "shouting" (that is, typing in all caps) in an online forum. For older Natives, meeting new people to date and even one's spouse online seems natural. It seems inevitable that this will soon filter down to finding friends at all ages.

Digital Natives Are **Evolving** Differently *Peripheral, emergent behaviors*
One of the most intriguing things about the Digital Natives' e-lives is that they are continually evolving and the kids are continually creating new behaviors that facilitate their lives. Natives have learned to type messages with the keys on their cell phones, in their pockets, at quite reasonable rates of speed. They have learned to manage 20 conversations in 20 instant messaging windows simultaneously, while still doing their homework in their laps. ("I don't understand how she does it," says her mother. "She tells me 'It's easy.'") When instant messaging, the two letters "OK" take too long to type—believe it or not—so the Natives use just a "k." The sociologist Mimi Ito and others have observed new social behaviors emerging among Japanese Digital Natives, such as leaving home with no fixed meeting place and arranging their meeting on the fly on their cell phones.

Digital Natives Are **Growing Up** Differently *Exploring, transgressing*
Finally, online (a term that has been already outmoded by *wireless*—we need, and the Digital Natives will no doubt invent, a new one) is one of the key places, in addition to home, school, and physical meeting places, where the Digital Natives are growing up. Like all young people, they explore, transgress, and test the limits in each of their spaces. Yes, pornography is easier to find online than under someone's bed, but what does that mean? We adults ought to be understanding and thinking about these coming-of-age behaviors on the Web so we can help our kids navigate their new world.

෫ ෫ ෨ ෨

FOLSOM LAKE COLLEGE LIBRARY

Those are just some of the many changes going on today—what do they all signify? More than anything, I think, they signify that the Digital Native generation is moving ahead in its own direction. It's headed, inexorably (although some of its members will move faster than others), to incorporating its birthright—digital technology—into its life in new, often unexpected ways.

And while some Digital Immigrants are afraid of the new technology, and others may question its value, the Natives are never going back, en masse, to the old ways.

Yes, there will be some Digital Natives who still hand-write letters, just as there are musicians who play 16th century music on old instruments. But letter writing in longhand is a thing of the past, like it or not. So are things like holding only one conversation at a time, looking people in the eye to know if you trust them, shaking hands as the final rite of a deal, hiding porn under the mattress, keeping information to oneself for personal status, paying for music, buying without easy comparison shopping, games where you don't create parts yourself, dating that isn't technology mediated, reputations based on status rather than performance, excuses for not having information, and many, many other things. Get used to it.

In a very short time technology has changed an entire generation's behavior radically, and it behooves all of us who are not from that generation but whose daily lives involve interaction with them, such as parents and teachers, to learn as much as we can about the new behaviors.

(If you are someone who doesn't think behavior *can* change that fast around technology, try to think back to how quickly, when telephone answering machines first appeared, the norm went from "It's rude to have an answering machine" to "It's rude *not* to have an answering machine.")

Today norms and behaviors are changing *much* faster than in the past, because the technology changes rapidly and the Digital Natives are programmed to—and *want* to—keep up with it. For adults, some new Digital Native behaviors may be worth immediately imitating and adopting (blogging, for example), others will seem really strange (online dating, perhaps), and others will forever be out of reach and impossible to adopt given their pre-digital "accents" (for example, one-handed typing on a cell phone in your pocket).

But there is a new, emerging, *different* form of life out there that the Digital Natives are creating for themselves. If you are a parent or educator, the one thing you can be absolutely sure of is that you ignore it at your peril!

7

Young Minds, Fast Times

The 21st century digital learner

Published in Edutopia

A few years after I began speaking to educational groups I decided that it was important to add "ground truth" (a military term meaning the perspective of the people closest to the action) to my talks. I wanted educators to hear not only what I—a 65-year-old—thought, but to hear what their own students thought, in general and about my ideas. I wanted to get students and their educators talking with each other about how today's young people learn. So I began adding panels of local students to my presentations whenever possible. The panels turned out to be more successful than I'd ever hoped or dreamed. This essay is their story.

෬ ෬ ෨ ෨

I give presentations to educators at every level, all around the world. All of the teachers are earnestly trying to adapt their educational systems to the 21st century. During my talks, however, I typically look out at oceans of white hair. Never—I can't even say rarely—is a kid in sight or invited to the party.

It is a measure of the malaise of our educational system that these old folk—smart and experienced as they may be—think they can, by

One teacher queried, "Do computers cut you off from the world?" Not at all, said an excited student: "We share with others and get help. Technology helps—it strengthens interactions so we can always stay in touch and play with other people. I've never gone a day without talking to my friends online."

One California high school served up a dose of common sense: "Kids grew up around computers. They love them. Their computers are their second teachers at home." A student in West Virginia offered this nugget: "If I were using simulation in school, that would be the sweetest thing ever!"

More than half of all secondary school students are excited about using mobile devices to help them learn; only 15 percent of school leaders support this idea.

Blah, Blah, Blah

OK, so kids love computers. They all agree on that. There's another thing they agree on: No matter where I go in the world—the United States, Canada, Europe, Asia, Australia, or New Zealand—students are mind-numbingly bored in class. Listen up:

"I'm bored 99 percent of the time." (California)

"School is really, really boring." (Virginia)

"We are so bored." (Texas)

"Engage us more." (Texas)

"[My teachers] bore me so much I don't pay attention." (Detroit)

"Pointless. I'm engaged in two out of my seven classes." (Florida)

"The disconnect between what students want and what they're receiving is significant," said Julie Evans, CEO of Project Tomorrow, which tracks youth culture. "Student frustration is rising."

I've heard some teachers claim that this is nothing new. Kids have always been bored in school. But I think now it's different. Some of the boredom, of course, comes from the contrast with the more engaging learning opportunities kids have outside of school. Others blame it on today's "continuous partial attention" (CPA), a term coined by Linda Stone, who researches trends and their consumer implications. Stone describes CPA as the need "to be a live node on the network," continually text messaging, checking the cell phone, and jumping on email. "It is an always-on, anywhere, anytime, anyplace behavior that involves an artificial sense of constant crisis," she writes. "We pay continuous partial attention in an effort not to miss anything."

CPA differs from multitasking, which is motivated by a desire to be more efficient and typically involves tasks that demand little cognitive processing. We file and copy while we're talking on the phone and checking email, for instance.

Is this really new? I don't think so. In fact, I think it has always been the case. Excluding emergencies, or other experiences in which one's adrenaline is flowing, humans typically always have multiple things on their minds. Still others attribute the boredom to attention deficit hyperactivity disorder, but the T-shirt I recently saw a kid wearing in Rockefeller Center belies this theory: "It's Not Attention Deficit—I'm Just Not Listening!"

It's none of the above. If you believe the opinions of kids around the world (and you ignore them at your peril), the source of the problem is abundantly clear, and it's this: Today's kids hate being talked at. They hate when teaching is simply telling. They hate lectures and tune them out.

I've heard teachers argue that some subjects and topics need to have lectures, but, in truth, this is only a justification for the failure of those teachers to change how they teach. It is absolutely not true; there are other ways, in any discipline, to get students to learn exactly the same material without lectures—as well as without worksheets, something else the kids tell us they really hate.

There are better ways to help them learn, and students expect us, as the adults in the room, to know how to use them. They say, for example, "If you made it more interesting we would respond better." And, "If you give us a goal to get to, we'll get there."

Students universally tell us they prefer dealing with questions rather than answers, sharing their opinions, participating in group projects, working with real-world issues and people, and having teachers who talk to them as equals rather than as inferiors. Hopefully, this is useful information for teachers and other educators—and it is important that educators realize just how universal these opinions are.

Nearly two-thirds of secondary school students want to use laptops, cell phones, or other mobile devices at school.

"My Brain Is Exploding . . . "

For me, though, the best part of the student panels is always hearing the kids' answers to my final question. I ask about their experience that day and whether their soapbox proved useful. "How do you like being able to talk to your teachers and supervisors about your learning?" I ask. I truly love their answers:

"I like the fact that we become equals. Students do not get the opportunity that often to share their ideas. If students and teachers could collaborate, a lot more would get done." (Anaheim, California)

"A lot of students care—you just don't realize it." (Poway, California)

"Most of the time, the teachers are talking and I want to go to sleep. But now my brain is exploding." (Poway, California)

"Don't let this be a one-time thing." (Poway, California)

"I think it's important that you take time to see what we feel." (West Virginia)

"Now you know what we think and how we feel. Hopefully, that will go to the heart." (Texas)

"I waited twelve years for this." (Texas)

"I wouldn't have believed it if I hadn't seen it!" (Texas)

"As a general rule, you don't hear from kids unless they've gotten into trouble." (Anaheim, California)

"Both groups [teachers and students] can learn from each other." (Anaheim, California)

"If you don't talk to us, you have no idea what we're thinking." (Hawaii)

Clearly, the kids find it valuable to share with their educators their opinions on how they want to learn. Although skeptical, they hope those teachers and administrators who are trying to improve their education think so, too, and listen carefully to what the students have to say. Again, quoting the kids:

"It would be good if teachers have this conversation with us on the first day. But often, they don't change anything." (Texas)

"I hope this didn't just go in one ear and out the other." (Texas)

Have there been any quantifiable results in terms of real changes to the students' daily lives? It's hard (and probably too early) to tell, although I do know for certain that the panels have had an influence on the administrators in the audiences. Many superintendents have invited me back to do the talks and panels again for their principals and teachers. Australian administrators distributed a three-CD set of the kids' discussions to every teacher they supervise. My great hope is that, once modeled, these types of conversations will be repeated frequently in our schools, in the United States, and around the world.

Bottom-Up Input

After hosting dozens of these conversations, I realize one thing: We just don't listen enough to our students. The tradition in education has been not to ask the students what they think or want, but rather for adult educators to design the system and curriculum by themselves, using their "superior" knowledge and experience.

But this approach no longer works. Not that the inmates should run the asylum, but as 21st century leaders in business, politics, and even the military are finding out, for any system to work successfully in these times, we must combine top-down directives with bottom-up input. As the students have told me on more than one occasion, "We hope educators take our opinions into account and actually do something!" Until we do, their education will not be the best we can offer.

8

Blame Our Young? Or Use Their Passion!

We can do better than just lay the responsibility for solving our nation's problems on the backs of our kids

An unpublished op-ed

I wrote the following essay as an attempt to put some of my ideas into the mainstream press. I sent it to the New York Times, *the* Washington Post, *the* Los Angeles Times, *and others. No one was interested, but perhaps you will be.*

ೞ ೞ ೦ ೦

Barack Obama does it. Colin Powell does it. Newt Gingrich does it. Columnists and editorial writers have been doing it for years. Even professional educators do it.

What is it? First they trace our country's problems to education, and then they lay the blame squarely on the kids.

"Pull up your pants!" says Powell. "What you make of your education will decide nothing less than the future of this country," says

Obama in his recent address to students. And by the way (he implies), you're not living up to our expectations or meeting your responsibilities—or else I wouldn't need to give you this lecture.

You can read it in hundreds of columns in thousands of variations: if our country has no future, it's all our kids' fault. Why can't they work harder? Why can't they stay in school longer and get better grades? Why can't our kids be like the kids in Finland, Singapore, you name it? Why can't they stop our competitive decline by going into math, technology, science, and engineering careers? Come on, kids, step up and solve our problems! It's what I call the "discipline" approach to education. In a recent *Meet the Press* appearance, Gingrich used the word *discipline* almost a dozen times.

Unfortunately, the "discipline" approach to education (that is, external pressure, not self-discipline) is ineffective long term, unfair to the kids, and, most of all, counterproductive. It is unlikely to get us any of the things we really need, and, at worst, it will turn our kids off even further than they now are to formal education and learning. Because of this, all these attempts to reach young people by talking about "discipline" and "patriotism" have little effect.

A Better Way

There is, however, a different and much better way to approach and motivate our kids to learn. Not through *our* needs, but through the kids' own interests and passions. John Seely Brown of Xerox PARC and USC calls it "passion-based learning."

Nicolas Negroponte of MIT wrote me many years ago: "I believe that learning comes from passion, not discipline." Sir Ken Robinson, author of *The Element*, a worldwide best-seller about finding one's passion, agrees.

Our kids today are incredibly passionate, even our dropouts. If one were to ask them—which, incredibly, most of their teachers (and even most parents) never do—one would find passions ranging from the environment, to cars, to motorcycles, to space, to sports, to the Internet, to music, to dance, to medicine, to people, to coins, to history, to singing, to history, to nature, to animals, to programming and robots, to business, and lots of others. Recently on a bus I heard a kid who dressed and sounded like the quintessential gang member say to his friends: "I'm a real Civil War buff—ask me anything."

Given today's powerful new tools and enormous opportunities to learn about whatever one is passionate about via the Internet,

YouTube, Wikipedia, and such, our kids are getting their most important education (and the only one they really care about) after school, on their own time. Alone and with their peers, they are watching, reading, making, sharing, and, most of all, learning.

We do not capture even a tiny fraction of all this learning-related energy in our schools. In fact, it's the opposite—we turn it off, by telling our kids, in no uncertain terms, what they have to learn (the curriculum) and how they have to do it (no cell phone learning allowed, for example).

What if, instead, we asked the kids what their passions are and invited them to follow and use those passions as a gateway to all kinds of learning—learning that will help our country and the world.

Wherever this has been tried—in scattered public, private, and charter schools, and even MIT—it has been a resounding success. Kids flock to be part of something that allows them to follow their own interests.

A teacher said to me recently, "I spend so much time trying to put my own passion into my teaching; it just never occurred to me that each of my students has a passion too." They all do, and they're waiting for us to discover and use these passions. And when we do, we will get all the results we want, and more.

"Learn for the country?"—"No thanks." "Learn because there is something you love and are passionate about?"—"Where do I sign up?!"

9

To Educate,
We Must Listen

Reflections from traveling the world

I wrote this unpublished essay and posted it on my website upon return-ing from a conference in New Zealand. It needs, I believe, no additional explanation.

CR CR SO SO

*The cookies on my daughter's computer know
more about her interests than her teachers do.*

—Henry Kelly, President,
Federation of American Scientists

I have just returned from presenting a keynote address at the International Confederation of Principals Conference in Auckland, New Zealand, where nearly 2,000 principals from all over the world met to hear the latest information in their field. My topic was "Engage Me or Enrage Me," about how our failure to engage our kids in their education has been leading kids universally to boredom and disaffection.

To my total amazement, another of the featured speakers managed to give an entire one-hour talk about being a principal without even once ever mentioning students! And it suddenly became crystal clear to me why the efforts of so many leaders, from Messrs. Michael Bloomberg and Joel Klein in New York, to all the chief executives who want to be the "Education President," to politicians and school administrators around the nation and the globe, are failing and are going to continue to fail.

They ignore the kids.

Oh, the students are there, of course, administratively. And budgetarily. But today's educational discussions are only about two things: how to "reform the system" (for example, smaller schools, better management from principals, more highly qualified teachers, more parent involvement, and so on) and what we do "to" kids (for example, new reading or math programs, more or less technology, and so on). There is almost no discussion *with* students of who today's kids are and how they want to learn. (*Hint:* It may not be by being taught in the traditional ways!)

The reason we are failing to educate our kids is essentially that we have become afraid to talk to them.

Why this might be the case is understandable—many of our "Digital Native" students are truly ahead of us in terms of technology, and many others put up a tough cultural front that is often hard to break through. Most of today's teachers teach by delivering content, presenting and telling linear stories, one thing at a time, one size fits all, and in person.

Yet their students learn from being engaged, doing, game play, random access, exploring options, multitasking, having things personalized to them, and going online. So when dealing with their students, teachers often feel like immigrants who speak a different language. As one student put it, "There's so much difference between how teachers think and how students think."

But it doesn't have to be that way. I spend my time going around the world speaking to educators, and I typically include panels of local students in my talks. It is almost always the first time that any of them have ever been asked about their own education. They say a variety of things, from that they are generally "50 to 99 percent" bored, to that they love their best teachers (although they think most are not that good), to that they have to "power down" when they go to school compared to what they can accomplish on the outside. But they especially say they would like to be consulted more about their own education, because they have a lot to contribute.

Today's kids are not "little us's" as they were in the past, and to engage them we must treat them differently, telling them where we want them to go and letting them get there, rather than just pumping information into their heads. This generation is much better than we adults ever were at sharing and teaching each other, yet we take little or no advantage of this. Today's kids hate to be "talked at," yet most of our teaching time is spent "covering the material" via lectures. (Educators may tell you this isn't so, but the kids say differently. Says one fifth grader: "I'm bored almost all the time because the teachers just talk, and talk, and talk.") Kids say what they value most is discussion and hearing each others' opinions—teachers often complain there isn't time to do that and prepare for the tests.

It's not that there aren't other means to educate young people—there are. But we have become so locked into our "20 to 40 kids in a classroom" model that we generally consider no other alternatives. Combinations of peer-to-peer learning, tutoring, and newer technologies (as opposed to the 10-year-old ones that just got tested and got a bad rap) can make a difference, as more and more homeschoolers are finding every day. In fact, the most future-oriented and valuable part of our kids' education now happens not in school, but "after-school"—in computer and robotics clubs, on the Internet, in complex online games, in peer-to-peer sharing, in self-awareness and retention programs, and in many other non-school ways.

I continually remind educators that while in the past kids grew up in the dark intellectually and our role (and value) as teachers was to enlighten them, in the 21st century our kids grow up in the light, connected to the world by television, mobile phones, and the Internet long before they ever go to school. Sadly, rather than building, as we should, on their knowledge and connections, we instead cut off all their external links and, as they enter our school buildings, bring them back into darkness. For how long do we think students will put up with this?

I have seen elaborate rules and codes of conduct set up by administrators for students. But there need be only two rules for kids in school: Do your best every moment to learn, and do not disturb anyone else in the process. It should only be when you are breaking one of these rules that you are failing.

Much of the answer to our education "problem" lies, simply, in listening to our kids, whose opinions should be sought at all educational levels. Bright, articulate student representatives should be on all school boards, steering committees, and curriculum and methods planning committees. They should be testifying before legislatures and teaching in our teacher training schools. They know what they need and a good deal of how to get it.

Not that kids should "run the asylum." But today institutions everywhere, from corporations to the military, are discovering that maintaining a healthy balance of "bottom-up" management (that is, listening) with the old "top-down" management (that is, demanding) is a far better way to be successful. It is high time we stop hiding behind our teaching and administration desks, afraid of our own kids, and learn to dialog with them about their own learning. After all, isn't that what real education is all about?

10

Bringing the Future to School: The Prensky Challenge

Who will be the first to challenge rather than blame our students?

This "modest proposal" was posted on my website several years ago. I received enthusiastic responses from exactly three people, who all thought it a great idea and worth doing. One of those three, it turns out, does work for the National Science Foundation. So who knows?

◌ ◌ ◌ ◌

*I never teach my pupils; I only attempt to
provide the conditions in which they can learn.*

—Albert Einstein

I strongly believe that the fact that our kids are totally bored in school ("I'm bored 99 percent of the time" said one 10-year-old recently) and that they are not getting better grades, higher scores, or going into math and science careers at the rate we would like, is *our*—that is, educators'—fault, and not the fault of our students. Any educator who blames the kids rather than himself or herself (except in isolated cases) is in need of some catch-up education.

One of the biggest reasons kids are bored and don't succeed today is that in school we deny them their own future!

What do I mean by this?

Today, education is caught between two worlds. What do today's kids hear about in their lives? Bioethics (Terry Schiavo). Genomics (genetically altered foods). Space travel (the Mars project). Data security (identity theft). Rarely if ever are these subjects taught or explored in depth in our schools. Instead, the kids are offered a curriculum developed in, and based almost totally on, the past.

How much of what our kids learn today will they use in the rest of their lives? I maintain it's far less than 20 percent. Why? Because our education is almost entirely focused on what was, not what will be. And the past no longer informs the future as much as it once did. Even "thinking" skills such as logic, communication, and problem solving, that we do know will still be useful in the future, are today taught in contexts that are completely outmoded.

This emphasis on the past is what I call our "Legacy" curriculum." And while only a small portion at best is useful for our kids' future, it is the curriculum that provides the credentials kids need to move forward. A much more relevant "Future" curriculum—if kids get it at all—comes almost entirely after school—though gaming, Web surfing, science fiction reading, and other technology use such as mobile phones.

And while more and more forward thinkers recommend just giving up the Legacy curriculum (or rescuing from it only what is needed) and switching to more Future-oriented learning, most educators and parents are nowhere near being ready to do this. As a realist, I understand that it's *really hard* to change curricula. (One wonders how we ever got rid of Latin!) The problem for our kids, though, is that the Legacy curriculum now takes up 100 percent of their class time, so preparing for the future is totally crowded out (along with art and music)—to the students' total detriment.

So here's a proposal.

One way to reduce the time needed for the Legacy curriculum—and still keep the people who won't give it up happy—and to make time for more Future-oriented learning, is to get the kids to learn the Legacy stuff faster. Is this possible? I'm convinced it is.

Suppose that, at the beginning of the school year, we said to students—at any grade level, and at any level of preparedness—the following:

> We have prepared for you a second semester that is fantastic, and totally future oriented. We will teach you about space exploration, nanotechnology, genomics, proteomics, bioethics, quantum computing, and all the wonders of the coming world. You will learn to program your phones and iPods to their max. You will build robots that can compete and win prizes. You will read and discuss the best science fiction there is. Your instructors will include—virtually—famous people from all over the world, including famous scientists, game designers, cell phone makers, and so on. You will use technology such as 3D printers and Nintendo DSs. This will be by far the most exciting thing you ever saw in school (and possibly anywhere else).
>
> But here's the thing: In order to get this fantastic second semester, you, the students, have to learn the entire year's regular curriculum in just the first semester—and *all* of you must pass the standardized test that says you've learned it.
>
> To get you all to learn, those of you who are strong in whatever areas will need to help those who are weaker. You can organize however you like, and work together in groups of your own choosing as much as you want, in order to meet the overall goal, which is that *all* of you pass. Your teachers will be there to guide you as to what you need to learn, and provide whatever help they can that you ask them for. But the basic responsibility for every student's learning the material in just one semester will be on you.

Do you think any group of our students, if given this kind of strong carrot, worthwhile goal, and responsibility to meet that goal themselves, would be able to accomplish this?

I think *every* group would. And I'm looking for partners to (1) fund the "Future content" creation and (2) provide the students in order to try the experiment.

Want to help? I'm at marc@games2train.com. Thanks.

11

Open Letter to the Bill & Melinda Gates Foundation

There is one lasting impact
only you can make

I am very worried that, for all their good intentions, Bill and Melinda Gates' huge amount of education philanthropy will almost all go to waste in the long-term. This letter explains why.

ೞ ೞ ജ ജ

Having hundreds of millions of dollars to spend on educational reform is an awesome responsibility, a responsibility that I know you do not take lightly.

However it is not at all clear—especially in light of your initial efforts—where your vast sums of money will do the most good. I assume you are currently in the midst of great internal debates and discussions about this.

As someone who has been observing education—and students—carefully for a while, I'd like, with due respect, to add my voice to the discourse.

First, I'd like to offer a guiding principle. While there are a great many things you and your money *can* do for public education, most of these can also (and hopefully will, to the extent they are truly necessary) be done by other institutions over time, although perhaps at a smaller scale or slower pace.

I suggest, though, that there is at least one thing that *only* an effort of your magnitude, independence, and prestige can accomplish in the foreseeable future. And I suggest it is in this area (and there may be others, i.e., places where your money will accomplish something that could not get done otherwise) that you should be placing your main focus and biggest bet.

That said, what area is this?

In my view, the single hardest thing to do in American public education, the one thing that for a number of reasons can't and won't get done in the foreseeable future without your specific intervention, is *updating our public school curriculum for the 21st century.*

Why is this unlikely to get done in other ways? Curriculum control in the United States is incredibly fragmented. Districts and regions and states have strong, often widely differing opinions and degrees of freedom. But, in addition, there are many other groups with strong opinions and various degrees of control and/or veto power, including the Federal government (including and not including the Department of Education), the teachers, the unions, the subject-based associations, the curriculum commissions, the administrators, the parents, the pundits such as William Bennett, politicians at several levels, and the non-education professionals, especially, recently, our scientists. Surely there are others as well.

Because of this fragmentation, without a major intervention no single curriculum is likely to prevail, and little, other than small, incremental curricular change, is likely to happen in our lifetime.

Yet the need for curriculum reform is severe and pressing. In a time of unprecedented, dynamic, exponential, "hyper-change"—a time when our students' minds and hopes are uniquely focused on the future—our curriculum is almost entirely about the past. While there is no question that the past informs the future to some degree, we are currently in a situation where the past in our curriculum is crowding out the future almost entirely. If we are to prepare our children to be successful in the 21st century, this situation cannot continue. Learning about the future, including subjects like media literacy, programming, online collaboration and problem solving, genetics, proteomics, nanotechnology, bioethics, prediction, adaptation, and environmental science ought to comprise *at least* half of the curriculum.

While our current curriculum varies enormously from place to place, it is probably safe to say that the Pareto Rule almost universally applies: 80 percent of the curriculum's lasting value to the students comes from 20 percent of the content. So we need to assess *why* we teach the things we do, and to see if we can't teach those same fundamental things in newer, more 21st century–useful ways. As an ex–high school math teacher, I know, for example, that the same logical lessons that 2,000-year-old geometry is meant to teach can be taught in a much more future-thinking way through programming. Assuming this happens, no kid *needs* a second semester of geometry, and possibly not even an entire single semester, to be prepared for the 21st century. In Language Arts, along with the classics of fiction that kids are (and should be) taught, we ought to also be teaching the classics of *science fiction*—the literature about the future.

I'm sure some will agree with these (personal) views, and others will disagree. And that is precisely my point.

We cannot and will not reach consensus on a 21st century curriculum in the current fragmented environment without some major outside intervention.

I believe the only way for the fundamental, massive curriculum change we need to happen is for a group with the independence, prestige, and financial and marketing power of the Gates Foundation to provide political and social "cover" for such change. The Foundation can do this by creating and blessing a new "standard" 21st century "Gates" curriculum that blends the past or legacy content with future content, in a contemporary, different, and dynamic way.

Obviously it will be a massive undertaking to create such a curriculum, and there will be no way to force any school, district, or state to adopt and use it. But if it comes out well, and gets endorsed by the leading, most highly respected thinkers of our day—from science, from education, and from other areas—adopting the "Gates Curriculum" can become a politically safe and even forward-thinking thing for school boards and states to do.

- In this way, the Gates Foundation could have a similar or even greater effect than the Carnegie Commission in the 1970s, which had a huge impact on our higher education institutions. While those institutions may now again be ripe for change, the

Carnegie Commission was revolutionary in its time, producing an "astonishing volume of high-quality material" (according to an evaluation at http://cshe.berkeley.edu/publications/docs/ROP.Douglass.Carnegie.14.05.pdf). Although they were not successful at everything they undertook, "in a number of instances, the influence of the commission and council, and the bevy of affiliated scholars, was substantial" (same reference). Many of the commission's recommendations became close to universal in their adoption and application.

- Currently, I can't see any other organization besides the Gates Foundation—not even the federal government—with the ability to have the same influence and impact on the public school curriculum.

Of course there are many other pressing issues in public education besides curriculum. They include, among others, teacher quality and training, teaching methodology, class sizes, student relationships, using technology, and assessment. But of all the pressing issues facing public education, I think curricular reform is *only* one where the Gates Foundation could leave an indelible mark for the future *of which no one else is capable.*

Let me close by relating this to the current educational climate of worry over America's standing in international test rankings, particularly in science and math.

Those who think that the United States can compete on test scores with countries that can put a variety of pressures on kids that we cannot, are, I submit, badly mistaken. But that doesn't mean we are, or should be, losers in the global competition for talented people. In business it is well established that the way to win is not for everyone to compete with the same strategy, but rather for each player to select a strategy that maximizes its own competitive advantages. This view of business competition has been extended by scholars to countries as well.

So let us ask: What is America's competitive advantage in education? The answer, I believe, is, and always has been, *creativity,* not knowledge. Our longtime competitive advantage in the world is our people's continued ability to see things in new ways, to approach problems from different perspectives, and to produce new and successful solutions. It is on *this* world ranking, and not on test score rankings, that we should be striving to be (or remain) number one.

Encouraging and maintaining this creativity in our public school students should, I submit, be a key part of the new Gates Curriculum. Americans, it must be remembered, comprise only 4 percent of the world's population. Intelligence, however you measure it, is distributed equally among all peoples. So we in the United States had better be focusing on something the others aren't focused on to the same degree, i.e., best preparing and equipping our kids with the creativity to be successful in a dynamic, hyper-changing future (rather than on mastering the curriculum of the 20th century and before).

I submit that this is the task on which your hundreds of millions can be most wisely spent. I will be pleased to offer my further thoughts and assistance should they be requested.

Respectfully,
Marc Prensky

1. In order to bring our education into the 21st century and fully prepare our students for their future lives, what needs to be done? Why is it important to talk frequently with our students about how they learn and how we can best teach them? What are some ways we can do this on a regular basis?

2. What don't we still know about learning? Why is that important?

3. What are good *positive* metaphors for our students? For our teachers?

4. What assumptions should teachers make, if any, about the students they teach? What assumptions *shouldn't* they make?

5. Do educators really "turn out the lights" for today's students? In what ways? What could they do differently?

6. Is the Digital Natives/Digital Immigrants metaphor—first proposed in 2001—still relevant today? In what ways is it still useful? In what ways not?

7. Do students think differently from the ways their teachers do? If so, in what ways? Does it matter? Why?

8. What are the positive things about today's students' online lives? How can we best integrate those lives into our schools and teaching?

9. Students are often blamed for their (and our) educational problems. Is this fair?

10. Is the fact that our students do less well on international tests than in the past important? Why? In what other ways could we assess the strengths and weaknesses of our students?

11. What should philanthropists be doing to effect the most lasting and important changes in education?

12. Where is money that could be spent improving education being wasted?

PART 2

21st Century Learning, and Technology in the Classroom

12

The Role of Technology in Teaching and the Classroom

Published in Educational Technology

Finding the right perspective and language is extremely important, because how we view and talk about something often determines what we do with it. At one point I realized that although many people were talking about technology in education and in the classroom, few, if any, had precisely defined its role. One reason is that this is not easy to do, particularly in a few words. Yet doing so is crucial in order that we may use the technology correctly. So I tried to do it in the following essay.

ﬠ ﬠ ﬡ ﬡ

It has taken a while, but I think I have finally come up with a single, comprehensive and actionable statement of the role of technology in the classroom. This is crucial, because many educators are becoming confused and frustrated by the myriad approaches and ways of talking about technology's role.

Although much in 21st century K–12 education still needs to be figured out, such as creating a generally agreed-upon 21st century curriculum, one goal is, I think, now clear—the pedagogy with which our kids should be taught. Although it can be stated in many ways, the basic direction is away from the "old" pedagogy of teachers "telling" (or talking, or lecturing, or being the "Sage on the Stage") to the "new" pedagogy of kids teaching themselves with teachers' guidance (a combination of "student-centered learning," "problem-based learning," "case-based learning," and the teacher's being the "Guide on the Side").

Of course this pedagogy is not *really* new, except, at the moment, to many of our teachers. Every teacher and administrator is, currently, somewhere on a continuum between the old and the new paradigms. Our Herculean task is to move all of them, around the world, to the new pedagogy as quickly as possible.

With this view of our goal (while some may disagree, it is becoming generally and widely accepted) we can now proceed to define the role of technology:

> *The role of technology in our classrooms is to support the new teaching paradigm.*

That is, technology's role—and its only role—should be to support students teaching themselves (with, of course, their teachers' guidance).

Technology does not, and cannot, support the old pedagogy of telling/lecturing, except in the most minimal of ways, such as with pictures or videos. In fact, when teachers are using the old "telling" paradigm, adding technology, more often than not, gets in the way.

New Tools for Students

One reason that the pedagogy of students teaching themselves never caught on as the mainstream approach—although it has been advocated by many, certainly since Dewey and probably since Socrates—is that the available tools for learners to use just were not good enough. Until relatively recently all the kids had to teach themselves with were textbooks, the encyclopedia (if they had one), the library (when they had access, and if theirs was any good), and a few questions to a generally overworked teacher. This worked for some bright students, but not for most.

Today's technology, though, offers students all kinds of new, highly effective tools they can use to learn on their own—from the

Internet with almost all the information, to search and research tools to sort out what is true and relevant, to analysis tools to help make sense of it, to creation tools to present one's findings in a variety of media, to social tools to network and collaborate with people around the world. And while the teacher can and should be a guide, most of these tools are best used by students, not teachers.

From this perspective, a number of previously puzzling things become clear:

- Some school districts added technology (e.g., by giving laptops to all students), but did not find that the technology was helping the kids' learning, and so took it out ("Seeing No Progress, Some Schools Drop Laptops," *The New York Times*, May 4, 2007). This now makes sense—the district didn't first get all the teachers to change the way they taught.
- Many teachers resist being taught to use technology. This also makes sense—teachers *should* resist, because it is not they who should be using the technology to teach students, but rather their students who should be using it, as tools to teach themselves. The teacher's role should not be a technological one, but an intellectual one—to provide the students with context, quality assurance, and individualized help. (Of course, those teachers who love technology are free to learn and use it.)
- Students routinely "abuse" (from the teachers' point of view) technology in class, using it, as one professor says, as "the new spitball." This, too, makes sense—kids have in their hands powerful learning tools that they are being given no opportunity to use to learn.

Students around the world are resisting the old "telling" paradigm with all their might. When their teachers lecture they just put their heads down, text their friends, and, in general, stop listening. But these same students are *eager* to use class time to teach themselves, just as they do after school when they go out and use their technology to learn, on their own, about whatever interests them. Students tell us, successful schools (mostly charters) tell us, and even our most successful teachers tell us: the new pedagogy works.

So before we can successfully introduce technology into our schools, we have to take a prior step. We must get our teachers—hard as it may be in some cases—to stop lecturing, and start allowing the kids to learn by themselves. Instead of coming in with lesson plans that begin "Here are the three causes of [whatever], please take notes," they need to say "There are three main causes of [whatever it is]. You have 15 minutes to use your technology to find them, and then we'll discuss what you've found."

If we can agree that the role of technology in our classrooms is to support the "new" pedagogy of kids teaching themselves with the teacher's guidance, then we can all move much more quickly down the road of reaching that goal. But if every person continues to talk about the role of technology in a different way, it will take us a whole lot longer.

This is part of a larger effort I hope to undertake with other educational thinkers to standardize our pedagogical language around technology, so that we can all be working toward the same goals, and all be requiring the same things from our teachers and students. Not that my words are necessarily the right or best ones, but, if we are to make the changes we want in a reasonable time frame, it is absolutely key that we all speak the same language.

13

Backup Education?

Too many teachers see education as preparing kids for the past, not the future

Published in Educational Technology

I wrote this essay in reaction to "pushback" I was getting from many educators who, after my talks, told story after story about technology breaking down and students not having "backup" skills. I believe the point the essay makes is absolutely crucial to moving our children's education forward into the 21st century. I hope you agree.

ଔ ଔ ଊ ଊ

Adisturbing voice has emerged in the questions that teachers ask after my talks. Reacting to my discussing the need to delete things from the curriculum in order to make room for topics about the future, teachers almost invariably ask some version of the following: "But what if the technology breaks down? What will our kids do then?" For example: "The power went down in a store the other day and the workers couldn't make change." "Just the other day our bus broke down on the highway." "Didn't you read about the cyber-attack in Estonia?"

Teachers who ask these questions and voice these opinions often get applause from their colleagues in the audience, making them think they are right in holding these attitudes. But these questions make me (and the students on my panels) realize that we have a real problem.

Of course technology will break down. And *of course* some people may not know what to do until it's fixed.

So why is the teachers' attitude a problem?

It's a problem because what the teachers are really saying is this: "We don't trust the technology of today, or the future. We don't trust the world in which you kids are going to live. We believe the way we did it in our time was the 'real' way, the only reliable way, and that's what we want to teach you kids—'the basics.'" (That's why they all applaud the idiotic video showing people on a stopped escalator just standing there calling for help.)

Confusing "Methods" With "Basics"

Unfortunately, thinking that many of the things we have students learn and memorize—from the multiplication tables, to the long division algorithm, to making change, to the state capitals—are "the basics" is confusing the "best method" of the moment with what is actually important to know. The reason we memorized so many of these things in the past was only because there was no handy/speedy way to look them up. But the "best methods" to the basics change over time.

For example, telling time is a "basic." At one time the best method we had was the sundial. Now we all just strap a machine to our wrist.

Math "basics" are the meaning and proper use of addition, subtraction, multiplication, and division, not the methods (i.e., algorithms) we use to perform those functions. Currently our best method for math is a calculator that we always have easy access to (perhaps strapped to our wrists as well).

Communication, too, is a basic skill, with reading and writing merely the best methods of the moment. Now both reading and writing are both very *useful* methods, which, to be clear, I think we need to teach until better ways emerge for getting the same information. But once all books are recorded, the Web reads itself, and every child and adult has a text scanner in his or her cell phone that can read any printed text aloud, should we still spend all those years teaching our kids phonics?

Writing is merely a method for recording thoughts. Not long ago neat cursive penmanship was the best method we had for this, because it was faster than printing and universally legible. Now we have better methods, such as phones, recording machines, IM (instant messaging), and keyboarding. As our kids all get their own phones and laptops, do we really need to teach them the old ways?

"Backup" Education

What the teachers described earlier are advocating that we teach our kids is not "the basics," at all, but rather a "backup" education of old methods—ones that are now useful only in unlikely emergencies. Those who continue to teach kids things they need to know only when stuff breaks down are doing those kids an enormous disservice. There is rarely a need to go back to the old ways, even when technology breaks down. Typically we are inconvenienced a bit, then we fix what is broken and move on.

The real issue lies in the fact that by continuing to teach the "backup" stuff, there is no room to teach for the future. Within the working lives of our students, technology will become a billion times more powerful, likely more powerful than the human brain. What will serve our kids better in 20 years—memorized multiplication tables or fundamental knowledge of programming concepts? Long division algorithms or the ability to think logically and to estimate? The ability to write cursive handwriting or the ability to create meaningfully in multimedia? (And that's just for elementary school—the same applies to the higher grades as well.)

Irony

The irony is that by the time today's elementary students get to the workforce, many of the breakdown scenarios the teachers describe will be structurally unable to occur. Making change, for example, will likely be gone altogether, as cash is replaced by our automated cell phone wallets. And while the dystopic scenario of everything breaking down at once (and only those with pre-21st century skills surviving) may make a good movie, it is incredibly unlikely to happen. (If it does, we'll have larger issues than kids' not knowing the multiplication tables.)

Those teachers who want to give their kids a backup education can't understand or accept that the world of their students is diverging incredibly quickly from their own. They don't understand that their well-intentioned instinct to "protect" their kids actually has the opposite effect—it prevents their kids from learning what they need to know to succeed in the 21st century.

Obviously, not all teachers believe backup education is the right way to go. But enough do, judging from the applause I hear, to seriously put our children's future at risk. So if the issue of "backup" education comes up in your neighborhood, resist it with all you've got. Our kids' future depends on it.

14

Simple Changes in Current Practices May Save Our Schools

"Easy-to-do, high-impact" steps all teachers should take

Published in ETC Online Journal

I wrote this essay just after the 2010 Deepwater Horizon oil rig blowout off the coast of Louisiana, which continued gushing oil unabated for three months, eventually releasing 4.9 million barrels of crude into a thriving marine environment. No one knew at that time what the results would be (and we are still finding them out). It occurred to me that the disaster, while talked about in many of our classes, could have been made a much more visceral experience for all our students—one they would be unlikely to ever forget—with only some simple steps, actions that could have been taken by volunteers at minimal cost. This is what I call an "easy-to-do, high-impact" step. One can also think about such steps as "leveraged," that is, not just effective, but effective at low cost of both money and time (and, therefore, in that sense only, "easy"). I believe that there are a number of these highly leveraged steps that all teachers can and should take, and I identify some of them in this essay. I encourage readers to think of more.

෬ ෬ ෨ ෨

Here's an idea to get at least something positive out of the Gulf oil spill. What if volunteers (or BP, under presidential order) collected samples of the tar balls on the beaches, sealed them in plastic bags, and then shipped them to every school in America for all students to analyze in their science classes? We could even throw in some oil-covered sand and feathers for good measure.

Doing this would involve every school kid (and science teacher) firsthand in the problem. They would see and smell, for themselves, just what the spill is actually producing, rather than just hearing about it on TV. Their awareness, as citizens and scientists, would be greatly enhanced.

To make it easier for teachers unfamiliar with the details of petroleum and environmental sciences, the NSF and DOE could quickly create study guides and lesson plans. Students and classes who were moved by these lessons could then talk with students living near the Gulf Coast, via email or Skype, to understand the devastation even further. They could discuss solutions, start Facebook and other groups, and contact local scientists. Many students would be motivated to pursue environmental and other sciences further, and to join and become active in environmental movements.

That is what today's education should be: not just "relevant" or "authentic" (the current buzzwords) but real; not just preparing students for some test based on "standards" but actually dealing with the problems of our—and especially the students'—day.

It is ironic that—given the current insistence on curriculum and standards—any teacher who wanted to divert class time to dealing with perhaps the biggest environmental disaster in U.S. history might well fear being taken to task for doing so. Providing such "real" education, in many school systems, would require special administrative dispensation from the curricula.

And those curricula, in all subjects, are currently so overstuffed that teachers typically have no time to cover all of it during the school year. That leaves little or no time for studying real problems as they arise, for deep discussions of issues, or for students to explore their own interests and passions. For our kids' education to improve, serious curricular deletion and revision is required.

Yet, our broken education system is, I believe, fixable. Not just by rushing to start new charter schools and programs, an expensive solution that is unlikely to reach the numbers we need (i.e., 55 million) in a reasonable time. Currently, the number of students reached per year by all the best programs put together, including all charter schools, which includes KIPP, Harlem Zone, New Vision, Uncommon Schools, and others, and programs like Teach for America, NYC Teaching Fellows, and Teaching Matters, is less than 2 million, i.e., only 4 percent of what is needed.

And not by rushing to the "disruptive" approach of teaching through technology, championed by Clayton Christensen and others. Certainly this will eventually help, but creating technology that teaches, and teaches well, except for the most highly self-motivated students, is extremely difficult and has yet to be done broadly. For our mostly unmotivated "middle students," who are the source of most of our failures and dropouts, online learning has yet to emerge as a viable approach.

The best, fastest, least expensive, and most easily executable solution to our educational problems is to change what goes on in our current classrooms. This is not as hard as many make it out to be since most of our teachers are people of good will and high motivation. What we need to do is provide them with easily doable directions that they can all start using in September to increase student motivation and performance. In addition to making education real, let me suggest five others.

The first relates to student passions. Our kids are almost all intensely passionate about many things (not typically their school subjects), but their teachers are typically unaware of what those passions are because they rarely ask. This is an issue that matters enormously to students and can be addressed with almost no additional work on the part of teachers. All they have to do is, at the beginning of the year when they ask each student his or her name, ask them what they are passionate about, write it down, and remember it. Once teachers know their students' passions, they can group them by their interests, give them differentiated assignments, and address them with different, more relevant approaches. Students will get the important message that they are cared about as individuals.

A second motivating change is for teachers to greatly reduce the amount of "telling" they do, relative to the amount of classroom activities and "partnering." If properly directed, all students today are capable of learning things they need to know on their own (using books, libraries, or course technology when available) without all the explanations having to come from teachers directly. It is actually far less work for teachers—and far more motivating for students—to cover the required curriculum by creating guiding questions for students to answer on their own rather than by creating new lectures.

A third thing that can be done immediately is to begin each day or class by putting students in the right frame of mind for their daily learning by employing existing, proven, 5 to 15 minute "relaxation" tools. These types of videos and software, which have been shown to greatly increase student focus and concentration and reduce difficult behavior, could easily be made available by the DOE to all teachers.

A fourth simple and motivating change would be to connect all our students to peers around the world through such free tools as ePals. Even when there is only one computer in a classroom (almost always the case in the United States today) students can, one or two at a time, regularly connect with students across the globe. ePals is not only free, it is secure as well.

A final quick change with great motivating potential would be to allow, for instructional use, devices the students already, to an increasing extent, own, know, and love, i.e., cell phones. There is a growing movement of teachers and educators who support this; they are creating lessons for the curricular use of cell phones while figuring out ways to deal with potential student abuse. If not all students in a class have their own phones, a teacher can easily create teams of two or more students to share.

All of these things are doable this September. If implemented widely, they would change the face of American education, improving it greatly. There are many other things we could do as well. Making these relatively simple, student-focused changes would have much more effect on student success than requiring more advanced degrees for teachers or even implementing smaller class sizes (this becomes less of an issue once students begin partnering and learning on their own).

We should all support experimentation and innovation in education. But instead of just spending, and often wasting, billions of dollars to create things that are new, let's try harder to fix what we have that's already in place. Our kids, when properly motivated, are far more capable and creative than our critics give them credit for. Let's give all of them the motivation they need to work, create, and succeed.

15

The Longer View: Why YouTube Matters

Why it is so important, why we should all be using it, and why blocking it hurts our kids' education

Published in On the Horizon

It is often pointed out that the impact of many technologies is greatly over-estimated in the short term but greatly underestimated for the long term. Nothing illustrates this better these days, I believe, than YouTube, and short video in general. In a very short time, YouTube grew from nothing to enormous proportions and dominated the press. Yet already YouTube is "old news," eclipsed in many people's minds by Twitter and other, newer technologies. I believe that in the long run, the impact of short video will be enormous, replacing, in a great many instances, much of what we today do in text. This is why I believe we should start not just introducing video in our schools (as many are doing) but using it as ubiquitously as we do text, making sure that all our students are fluent on both sides of the camera. This essay, which garnered a "Highly Commended" award from the Emerald Literati Network, explains why.

ᘓ ᘓ ᘔ ᘔ

Our media mediate our social interaction.
When our media change our social interaction changes.

—Michael Wesch, Kansas State University

Video is the new text.

—Mark Anderson, consultant

One of the most exciting things about living in the 21st century is watching large societal and cultural changes happen right before your eyes. This is nowhere better illustrated than in the rapid rise of YouTube. (Twitter has been getting all the press lately; but its long-term import is, I think, far less.)

YouTube first launched in 2005, as a way for people to post video clips online. Who knew then that it would launch an entirely new type of communication, and that there would be such a hunger for it? I remember the email asking me to check out the videos my programmer had posted on this new site. I can't say I rushed to do it. Now I couldn't do my work without it—I include YouTubes in all my presentations. Watching YouTube now consumes a large portion of many young people's media time, often taking time away from broadcast or cable television.

The number of YouTube clips available to watch is staggering. At the start of 2010 the number is fast approaching 100 million, with roughly 150,000 new clips posted daily. (That's an additional 5 million clips per year. And that's assuming the rate stays the same; it will probably increase.)

[*Note:* I asked Mike Wesch when he thought You Tube might get to 1 billion videos. He replied:

> My best guess would be sometime in 2013 if we are considering public videos on YouTube. A wildcat search on YouTube gets you 313 million. . . . [The company] recently noted that they receive eight years of content on any given day, which suggests they receive about 1,000,000 videos a day. With the high growth rate, they may reach 1 billion by 2012, but certainly by 2013.

This does not include Facebook, though. If you wanted to count all videos uploaded to the Web, it would be worth considering the privately shared videos on Facebook (and on YouTube, which are not counted in the search results). Counting those, I think we may already be at 1 billion.]

Two-Way Communication

Perhaps the thing about YouTube that is least understood by people who do not use it regularly is that it is not just one-way, or one-to-many, communication; it is designed to be, and very much is, two-way. There are easy-to-use communication and feedback channels built in, including view counts, ratings, text posts to any clip, and in the ability to make and post "response" video clips, which often happens. Many users post ideas and opinions, looking for feedback, and many get large numbers of responses to their clips. Language students, for example, often post clips and get feedback from native speakers.

Quantity AND Quality

Both the quantity and the quality range of YouTube videos are breathtaking. In only the last four years more video has been created and posted than broadcast television created in its entire history. Particularly when you broaden the term "YouTube" to include the many specialized short video sites—Teacher Tube, School Tube, Big Think, TED, Hulu, and the many "how-to" video sites—you can find, in video, the entire range of human communication, from clueless kids babbling, to sophisticated discourse and dialogue, world-class creations, and deep debates and discussions. As the YouTube slogan, "Broadcast Yourself," indicates, lots of individuals are pointing a camera at themselves, many for the first time, and saying their piece. Many are young, though more and more are older people, such as geriatric1927 (aka the "Silver Surfer"). There are people making complex arguments (such as the weather woman who decries, in a YouTube, the math methodologies being taught in certain textbooks), and counter-arguments (such as a math professor's responses). There are bereaved people with the need to express and share their feelings and who find comfort in people's responses, and there are ranters and shouters. At its core, YouTube is human communication, in all its forms (except, for the moment, synchronous dialog, which requires only the simple add-on of voice and/or text).

"The New Text"

"YouTubes," i.e., short, mostly self-created video clips (as opposed to professional film or television) have become, in the words of consultant Mark Anderson, "the new text." They allow complex, multimedia communication to and from anyone with an online computer, and, more and more, a cell phone. This last is key because, given the current rate of uptake, there will soon be a cell phone available— either individually or shared—to almost everyone on the planet. Although some videos contain text, to get most of the message (even of the most sophisticated) you need only watch and listen. In many cases you don't even have to know English, as many videos have been translated, manually or automatically, or are self-evident without translation.

Key for Educators

Why is this new communication form—short, mostly self-created videos—so important for educators to understand? The answer is that a huge portion of the world's knowledge, especially new knowledge, is going *uniquely* into this form. There is unique video on practically EVERY subject. Banning or ignoring this work (as often happens in schools) is saying, in effect, "We don't want to give our students access to a large part of the world's knowledge."

That is clearly a tough and, I think, untenable position for educators to take.

What is most amazing (and, at the same time, alarming to many educators) is just how quickly this whole phenomenon has taken off. When people put the tools to create these videos in the hands of individuals, and created an easily accessible place to put them, as well as a relatively easy (although as yet still clunky) way to find them, no one had any idea how big the explosion would be. Who knew that there would be 150,000 people a day uploading videos they had made? Who knew that the desire to capture and share would be so great? I think this took everyone, even YouTube's creators, by surprise. But perhaps it shouldn't have.

Communicating Using Writing and Reading Is Hard . . .

What many people, particularly educators, often forget (or ignore) is that writing and reading—although they have enjoyed great success and primacy for several hundred years—are very artificial and unnatural ways to communicate, store, and retrieve information. As most teachers are aware, reading is a skill that is difficult, and often painful, to learn and master. Any cognitive scientist will tell you what a struggle it is to get our brains to do it (as opposed to seeing and talking, which come much, much more naturally to humans). "Reading does not just happen," says University of California–Davis neurology expert Kathleen Baynes. "It is a terrible struggle." Even after hundreds of years of learning to teach it, a great many of our students (although they can watch and listen quite well) still have difficulty with reading and writing.

As a result, a great deal of our school time is devoted to training young people to use written media—first to decode the squiggles and then to extract meaning. And still, aside from our top-tier students, we are only marginally successful at it. Many countries in the world do not even attempt to make their non-elite students written-word literate. Those like us, who do try, find the task of teaching people to read and write daunting, and the task of getting people, once they have learned, to continuously use and improve those skills (i.e., to be lifelong readers and writers) even harder. We have a remarkably high percentage of "functionally illiterate" in the United States—some claim it is as much as 40 percent.

. . . But New Media Make It Easier

But that doesn't mean, of course, that all these people have stopped communicating. Rather (and this is a hard one for many to swallow) a large part of our population has already switched to media easier than reading and writing for almost everything. As noted, speaking and listening are much more "native" to the human brain. Now that we have technological alternatives, written communication, except in certain areas, is rapidly on the wane.

The evidence is everywhere. Written letters have been mostly replaced by phone calls. Most news is obtained from listening to people on TV. Even sophisticated arguments, such as Al Gore's message about global warming (*An Inconvenient Truth*) reach far more people via movies (i.e., listening and watching) than via books. Printed news that was once almost completely text—even the *New York Times*—is increasingly presented via graphics, "op art," online simulations, and news games. Magazines—especially text magazines—have lost much of their readership. Newspapers, large and small, are shrinking and going out of business. And even the Internet, which, to a certain extent, brought reading and writing back into vogue through Web pages and blogs, is fast moving to short-form video, i.e., to YouTube. Much of the written communication on the Web has moved to tiny forms such as Twitter, and these forms are likely to soon be replaced by voice and/or video as well.

This massive rejection of reading and writing—and substitution of other media—is, of course, not the case for the top 10 to 20 percent of our population (which includes almost all teachers). But it certainly is true for the remaining 80 percent.

The Future of Reading and Writing?

So what do we do? Should educators, and society, continue to struggle—valiantly but mostly in vain—to make every person in our society literate, in the old, reading and writing sense? Or should we accept that that's a war we won't win and move on to a different, and more useful, goal?

> Warning: *If you are a person who is tied, body and soul, to reading and writing as the form of communication, don't—repeat don't—read this. Skip to several paragraphs down. Read on only if you are open to new points of view.*

Although it is a very difficult thing for many educators and other people to hear and face, and strange as it sounds, the truth is that for most people in the 21st century reading and writing are *not* the best ways to communicate their thoughts and ideas. In fact, for the large majority of 21st century Americans they are rarely used, and not even truly necessary skills, and are quickly on their way to becoming even less so. Let me illustrate.

What communication materials do most Americans access today? News? Video is fine. Work- or school-related material? Video does it equally well. Instructions, contracts, or legal papers? Someone trusted explaining these to you on video is probably better than trying to read them yourself. Stories? Recorded versions of the text, or movies telling the same story are (except possibly for purists) equally good substitutes. Training? Learning? Video often does the job better. Books? A Kindle or other device will read them to you. Other written pages you really want to understand? A scanner can easily read them to you (you can currently buy this technology in a pen, and it will soon be a part of our phones). Signs? Most have moved to symbols. Place names? Again, a small device that can scan at a distance can do the job just fine. Map reading? GPS and voice technology have pretty much solved that. Searching for information? Currently tougher, perhaps, without reading, but with voice to text and text to voice soon it won't be. Email? You can already hear it read. Even voting decisions are now made based almost completely on watched and spoken communication (i.e., speeches and TV commercials) and not (except for that small, top percentage of people) on reading. Bemoan this if you will, but it's the truth.

And writing is even less widely used. Think of the average, non-college-educated person, once he or she leaves school. Aside from signing their name occasionally, what in life do they need to write? Not a whole lot that couldn't be communicated by voice, video, and pictures. A shopping list? Products already exist to record voice memos and shopping lists by talking to your refrigerator. A description of something? Voice is generally fine, and illustrations make it even better. An evaluation or form to fill out? Can be done on a touch screen with picture cues. A report? Record audio or video. The great advantage of audio and video over writing is that *anyone* can do it, i.e., anyone can stare at a mic or camera and talk. And increasingly, almost everyone does.

Whom Does It Serve?

So whom does it serve to have so many of our students struggle so hard (and typically unsuccessfully) for years to get something cogent down on paper, versus the option of learning to carefully present their thoughts in other media with which they are more comfortable and have more mastery? Are we spending all this time and energy teaching reading and writing just so that people can fill in forms and job applications? And if so, wouldn't it make more sense to just change those?

Recently, I had a conversation with a soft drink delivery person, who carried a small handheld computer on which he checked off items delivered, and printed out his customers' receipts. "Do you need to read and write for your job?" I asked him. "No," he said, "that's not important." "What is important?" I asked. "Talking," he said. "Good talkers always do well."

Compared to reading and writing, we hardly focus on that at all.

There remains, of course, a relatively small group of people, in certain professions, populations, and parts of society, for whom written literacy *is* important, and will clearly remain so for the foreseeable future. But that group is quite tiny relative to the number of people on the planet. And, importantly, *it no longer creates two classes, given that non-readers-and-writers have increasingly universal access to other communication tools.* It may be no different than those who can and can't speak a foreign language—there are many other ways to access the same material.

What to Do?

What does this mean for school? It probably means, for one thing, that (again as strange as it sounds) we should stop focusing on literacy, as in reading and writing (or, worse, literacies—an oxymoron), and focus, rather, on *communication of ideas.* How do we put ideas out there, clearly and succinctly, for other people, and how do we take them in? This is what we want our students to be good at, whatever medium they use.

Increasingly, people with things (even sophisticated things) to say, and intellectual arguments to make, are choosing non-written media. They are putting their thoughts and ideas into video (and other media, such as serious games) rather than writing, and sharing them on sites such as TED.com, bigthink.com, and even YouTube. Today, when searching, if one does not perform a separate video search in addition to a Google search, one misses vital information. (This despite the fact that the top YouTubes do come up in a Google search.) What might one miss? Speeches and presentations by Nobel Prize winners or key business executives, for example. Even a YouTube search is no longer enough. One needs to use a dedicated engine, such as blinkx.com, fooooo.com, truveo.com, pixsy.com, vizhole.com, that searches multiple video sites. (This is only temporary. Search will soon be integrated across media.)

Use Your Phone

Today, more and more cell phones can retrieve and play video—soon almost all phones will. This puts the 100 million videos on YouTube, TED.com, Teacher Tube, School Tube, Big Think, Wonderhowto, Ehow, Monkeysee, and other useful sites in your pocket, purse, or backpack all the time—available whenever you want or need them. Because much of this new video is talking heads, it works surprisingly well on the small screen—much better, in fact, than large volumes of text. As we become increasingly able to take and send (to one individual or a few) and upload (to many or the world) from our personal devices, why would we ever choose to send a written message? (Of course there are reasons for *some* people. But I'm talking about *most* people.)

The Anthropology of YouTube

One person who has been carefully observing YouTube is anthropologist and professor Michael Wesch, of Kansas State University. He has certainly opened my eyes, via his YouTubes and talks (many of which can be found, of course, on YouTube), to short video's true meaning and power. I strongly recommend everyone search for, and look at, his work.

What Wesch has principally helped me understand is the *extent* to which short video is a new way—perhaps *the* new way—to communicate, to share ideas, opinions, emotions, humor, parody with people around the world.

Scale

One of the most amazing things about YouTube is how easily it scales from tiny to enormous audiences. One can aim to reach only a few people (Wesch estimates that a high percentage of the videos on YouTube are designed for, and reach, under 100 people), but one can also aim for, and reach, thousands, hundreds of thousands, or millions of people. There are particular ways—documented by Wesch and his students—of going about creating "viral" videos that will reach numbers in the higher ranges. Before the advent of YouTube, Wesch's own anthropological ideas might have reached hundreds of people (i.e., his students), and perhaps several thousand in his life-time. His books might have reached tens of thousands, perhaps hundreds of thousands if successful. But his YouTubes can, and already have, reached an audience of millions. Some YouTubes (e.g., certain songs and dances) move incredibly rapidly around the world, engendering version after version, parody after parody—not just imitation, but reinterpretation and commentary. There are already YouTubes with over one billion views. Someday soon there will be a video—perhaps a phenomenal soccer play mashed up with a highly popular song—that will be seen by almost everyone on the planet.

Many people, including a growing number of teachers and intellectuals, have already decided they can reach people better with their ideas (or reach different people) through short videos on sites like Big Think and TED than through print.

Issues With YouTube

But, of course, there are issues. Mostly they involve sorting out the good and worthwhile from the bad and "to be avoided." Just as with all other media, there are "lowbrow" YouTubes, some with objectionable images and foul language. Few want this to become the main use of the medium, so people are quickly working out ways of automatically identifying "adult" material, in order to be able to label it, and flag it before one can see it, so that people can make appropriate choices. Already, today, many "adult" YouTubes are preceded by a disclaimer about their content.

As writer Clay Shirky points out, YouTube does not have a "content" problem, but rather a "filter" problem. The fact that we have not yet created very good automated filters that can evaluate a video by its content, or even by the words in it, is a major issue. But there are a lot of very smart people working hard on this problem, and useful, continuously improving solutions will, no doubt, soon emerge.

Making the Tradeoffs Correctly

There is a lot of YouTube that is just one not-so-interesting person talking (typically, to less than 100 watchers). And, as we just noted, YouTube has some objectionable material, both visual and spoken (just like all our media in a free society). Does this justify banning YouTube in our schools?

To answer this question one must also look at those negatives against the positives of YouTube for learning, and evaluate the trade-offs. Among the positives of YouTube—i.e., its learning benefits—are:

- An immense number of teaching videos, where someone who knows something teaches it to others. These have been created by teachers, by people in various jobs and professions, and by students and other young people. Topics range from "Using Web 2.0 to Teach Languages" to "Students Teaching Students Math." It would be foolish to ignore the medium of video as a powerful learning tool for today's youth. It is, in fact, mostly how they learn on their own, and one can, actually, learn entire new professions (such as how to be an online artist or developer) this way.

- A wealth of useful explanatory video on practically EVERY subject. A psychology teacher recently wondered if there were any videos of Freud's theories of the mind—there were, to his surprise, many.

- Video-based learning matches many (if not most) students' preference. Today's young people generally prefer video to reading as a way of learning.

- The job of *finding* good, useful video can be a part of students' learning. The same psychology teacher mentioned above decided to give points for the best videos found by students, rather than searching for them himself. He had useful responses within 10 minutes of posting the request, and found it more useful to have the students be the "quality filters" than himself.

- The ability for students to see, hear, and learn from top experts in any field. This increasingly includes Nobel Prize winners, top politicians, award-winning journalists, Supreme Court justices, etc.

- The ability for students to research and view the huge and growing number of primary-source, historical videos available, such as the anti-Nazi propaganda films made by Walt Disney during WWII.

- The ability for teachers to mentor, coach, and guide students through the process of viewing and reviewing YouTube videos, and to help students separate out what is true and useful from what is merely "there."

Many school districts and educators never even make the trade-offs before heading straight to a ban. The truth is the positives of video sites for education far outweigh the negatives (and, in addition, those negatives can be addressed through other means than bans, such as requiring students to turn off their computers if something inappropriate shows up on the screen). To use only the negatives to justify banning YouTube and other video sites (except, of course, for porn sites) is to disregard the huge benefits that these sites bring for student learning.

Using Video to Share Teachers' Successes

Ironically there is another group for whom YouTube-style video offers a fantastic potential solution, and that is teachers. For a variety of reasons—mostly generational—teachers typically do a very poor job of sharing their successful approaches, lessons, and pedagogies. This slows down tremendously the process of learning from each other.

Time and again teachers have shared with me great stories about good things they have done—things that it would be really helpful for other teachers to hear. Because writing (especially writing well for others) is such an effort, these stories are almost never documented in written form and posted (and thus made available to others via search). But all it would take to make this material available is for the teacher (or their student) to point a video camera (or cell phone) at themselves and talk for thirty seconds, telling the same story they told me. They could then either upload that story as is, or if they chose, they could augment the story with comments from students, and even a shot of the class if appropriate. (It's even becoming child's play to fuzz out faces if necessary.) The entire process of making and uploading such a sharing video, once one had a bit of experience, would take less than five minutes, and it could, potentially, reach, and influence, millions of teachers around the world. There are some teachers who are already doing this—there are some shared videos by teachers on using Web 2.0, for example. But this is something that *all* teachers—including college teachers—should be (and, in the future, I predict, will be) doing.

Speeding It Up

One might, of course, ask the question: "Where will the time come from for people to watch all these videos and communicate in these ways?" Some of it will certainly come from reading less, but, for many young people, it will come from the substitution of watching videos for watching broadcast TV. I have talked with teenagers who already watch no TV at all—but lots of YouTube. As online video expands to include things previously findable only on the networks, as it is already doing on Hulu, that substitution will only increase.

And, it turns out, we can also watch it faster. With tools that are very likely *already on your computer,* much video can be watched at fast-forward speeds, without changing the pitch of the voices. These incredibly useful tools are, for some reason, not highlighted, but buried deep within Microsoft Windows Media Player. To try them, when you are watching any video file in the Windows Media Player, hit "Ctrl-Shift-G" to speed the video up, "Ctrl-Shift-S" to slow it down, and "Ctrl-Shift-N" to go back to normal. You can also find a slider control for more precise adjustment. (Right click to access the menus.) A speedup of about 1.4 to 2 times faster seems to work best for video. It is also possible to slow any videos down for those whose comprehension is less good, or for understanding people speaking quickly or with accents. I have been arguing for years that these controls should be built into all video players, and hopefully, they, and other useful tools, will soon appear in other places. Sadly, they still do not exist on YouTube—but one can always, using a tool (such as *RiverDeep*) capture the online video as an .avi or .wmv file and play it through the Windows Media Player.

The Bottom Line: Media Are Changing

Mainstream media do not last forever—they get supplanted whenever it is deemed better by users to do so. A thousand years ago writing supplanted memory, over Socrates' bitter objections. Today, a new and important change is taking place. In only a few decades, television and cell phones have penetrated far further around the globe than the written word has in a millennium. YouTube, and short video in general, has, in a very short time, become a key medium for sharing and finding more and more sophisticated information of all kinds.

No one—least of all me—expects writing and reading to disappear any time soon, particularly among the intellectual classes. But as technology advances, other media are likely to take over the mainstream. This may be a change, but since little or no information is lost, it is hard to justify labeling it a "bad" one. Rather, it is only the march of progress, as information and communication changes forms (i.e., clothing) to suit the current world. Because, as McLuhan said, the medium is the message, this will bring other changes as well, to which we should remain alert.

I would expect that in the coming years, large numbers of additional video sites (along with other, more interactive forms) will blossom, containing most or all of the kinds of useful information that is now available mostly (or entirely) in print. In the education world, this will likely include student-created, teacher-reviewed curriculum-related videos and presentations that are available to all, and whose breadth and quality rapidly improves with time.

Educators who are still willing to deny or restrict their students' access to a major communications medium—one that is filled with highly relevant educational information (and is already, although still in its infancy, embraced and used by many top thinkers to spread their ideas)—now fall squarely into that shrinking camp of people who think that the only way to protect their students from the future is to deny it to them. That seems pretty counter-educational to me.

16

Beyond the Lemonade Stand

Economics and business lessons for a 10-year-old from a computer game

Published in Don't Bother Me Mom—I'm Learning

The experiences of my best friends' two sons featured prominently in my own developing understanding about the behavior of young people, and particularly about their learning from video and computer games. I was close to both boys from birth, and I spent a large amount of time over many years watching both of them play their increasingly complex games and talking with them often about what they were doing and why. A great deal of what I learned found its way into my book Don't Bother Me Mom—I'm Learning, *which is about, as its subtitle indicates,* How Computer and Video Games Are Preparing Your Kids for 21st Century Success—and How You Can Help. *This essay describes one of my experiences.*

ର ର ଚ ଚ

I was surprised when I heard 10-year-old Tyler talking with his 13-year-old brother about "firing" someone. "What's up with that?" I asked. Plenty, it turned out.

Tyler had come upon the massive multiplayer online game *RuneScape,* (www.runescape.com) and had started playing it. Like many other games of its genre, *RuneScape* is a fictional online world in which players quest, battle, trade, and earn treasure. They do so by mastering a variety of skills, such as mining, smelting, spell casting, and crafting objects, such as swords, helms, and charms. Ore and objects can be sold and traded, and finished objects can be used in quests, which can bring in additional treasure. *A typical in-game mini-economy.*

Tyler wanted to get really rich in the *RuneScape* world. But after playing alone really hard for a while, he realized that to get there he would need partners. "It takes too much time to get good at everything—mining, smelting, crafting, enchanting, and questing," he told me. "So I got my friends to play too. I smelted and crafted, and each of my friends did one of the other things." *Hmm . . . Sounds like an economics lesson on the Supply Chain and Division of Labor . . .* Does Tyler know those terms? No. But he certainly understands the concepts!

As a result of his game playing this lively fifth grader understands other key economic concepts as well. He patiently explained to me that ores sell for more once they're smelted into bars, and even more after they're crafted into objects. *Why that's . . . Value Added!*

"I made a big business mistake once," the 10-year-old candidly admitted during our interview. (Yes, I had to arrange and book with him my 15-minute interview, sandwiched between his school, game playing, soccer, chess, basketball and homework commitments.) "I decided to make steel helmets to sell," he said, "but I didn't research that the buyer already had lots of steel helmets. It turns out the more they have in stock, the less money a thing is worth." *Supply and Demand!* Once again, Tyler has mastered a concept without understanding the term—just the opposite of what typically happens in school!

"Our team wanted to make lots of money and really improve," Tyler continued. "Everyone had a job to do." *Business structure!* "One person held the money and everyone got paid." *Control!* "I had to find jobs for people, like mining, smelting, selling, and finding things to buy." *Full employment! Vertical integration!*

"So what about the firing?" I asked? "Well," said Tyler, "this one team member was supposed to take all the weapons and armor we made him, go on quests, and bring us back treasure to put in the community pot—we were all pooling our earnings." *Wealth creation! Capital building!* "But this guy just went off on the quests and kept the treasure for himself." *Corruption!* "He really didn't need our help and didn't use it. He was doing everything alone. He wasn't helping us and he wasn't doing his job. So I had to fire him." *Management!*

"How'd you do it?" I asked? "I said to him: 'You seem to be fine on your own, so I think you should *be* on your own,'" explained Tyler. He also revealed to me that he had agonized for days over whether to do it, and what to say, before having the conversation. *Making difficult decisions. Ethical behavior. Communication. The loneliness of command!*

"How'd he take it?" I inquired? "He was shocked, and he got upset. But I felt really sad, so I hired him back." *Compassion!*

"Did you ever think about giving him a warning?" I asked. "Not that time—but I should have. I will next time!" *Management training!*

So, from his enjoyable computer game, young Tyler has learned (without knowing it) the concepts of Supply Chains, Division of Labor, Value Added, Supply and Demand, Business Structure, Control, Full Employment, Vertical Integration, Wealth Building, Capital Acquisition, Dealing with Corruption, Making Difficult Decisions, Ethical Behavior, Good Communication, The Loneliness of Command, and Compassion. He even picked up some useful Management Training along the way.

This is economics and business learning for a 10-year-old that goes light-years beyond the "lemonade stand" example we taught our kids with in the past!

And, despite their enormous value, these lessons are not even the most important thing Tyler has learned from *RuneScape*. He and his friends play the free version of the game, which lacks the additional levels, subtleties, and bells-and-whistles of the ten-dollar-per-month version. When I asked him, since he liked the game so much, why he didn't just subscribe, he replied: "It would be too addictive, and my mom would get mad. I wouldn't get my money's worth." *The deepest economic lesson of all!*

(P.S.—None of this is made up!)

17

Types of Learning and Possible Game Styles

Published in Digital Game-Based Learning

I put this chart together for my first book, Digital Game-Based Learning. *It has been used by many, including the U.S. military, to help design educational games that work.*

ca ca so so

"Content"	Examples	Learning Activities	Possible Game Styles
Facts	Laws, policies, product specifications	• Questions • Memorization • Association • Drill	• Game show competitions • Flashcard-type games • Mnemonics • Action, sports games
Skills	Interviewing, teaching, selling, running a machine, project management	• Imitation • Feedback • Coaching • Continuous practice increasing challenge	• Persistent state games • Role-playing games • Adventure games • Detective games

"Content"	Examples	Learning Activities	Possible Game Styles
Judgment	Management decisions, timing, ethics, hiring	• Reviewing cases • Asking questions • Making choices (practice) • Feedback • Coaching	• Role-playing games • Detective games • Multiplayer interaction • Adventure games • Strategy games
Behaviors	Supervision, self-control, setting examples	• Imitation • Feedback • Coaching • Practice	• Role-playing games
Theories	Marketing rationales, how people learn	• Logic • Experimentation • Questioning	• Open-ended simulation games • Building games • Constructing games • Reality-testing games
Reasoning	Strategic and tactical thinking, quality analysis	• Problems • Examples	• Puzzles
Process	Auditing, strategy creation	• System analysis and deconstruction • Practice	• Strategy games • Adventure games
Procedures	Assembly, bank teller, legal	• Imitation • Practice	• Timed games • Reflex games
Creativity	Invention, product design	• Play	• Puzzles • Invention games
Language	Acronyms, foreign languages, business or professional jargon	• Imitation • Continuous practice • Immersion	• Role-playing games • Reflex games • Flashcard games
Systems	Health care, markets, refineries	• Understanding principles • Graduated tasks • Playing in microworlds	• Simulation games
Observation	Moods, morale, inefficiencies, problems	• Observing • Feedback	• Concentration games • Adventure games
Communication	Appropriate language, timing, involvement	• Imitation • Practice	• Role-playing games • Reflex games

18

On Being Disrespected

Response to email feedback from a reader

Published in Educational Leadership

All teachers certainly want and deserve respect from their students. However, all students want this too, so the ideas in this essay are extremely important for educators. One school administrator declared, after a recent talk I gave, "I'm going to begin all my sessions from now on with a discussion of mutual respect."

ෆ ෆ ෩ ෩

Respect.

We all probably think that we have it for our students. And we certainly think that they should have it for us. But do we? Do they? I am increasingly convinced that mutual *disrespect* lies at the root of many of today's classroom difficulties.

The issue was brought home to me in a personal way. In December 2005, I was privileged to have an article accepted in *Educational Leadership.* Titled "Listen to the Natives," the article presented many new ideas about educating kids in the 21st century.

I received several email responses from readers. Many were positive, but just as many disagreed with some of my points. I certainly don't mind criticism—I write to discuss new ideas and promote new thinking—and I certainly don't expect every reader to agree with me.

But one day an email arrived in my inbox, which I gathered was from a group of school administrators. There was no salutation. "Your sales pitch reminds us of silicon snake oil," it read. "Sorting data without context fuels ignorance."

Those two sentences hit me hard. I spent a great deal of time thinking about whether, and how, to respond. Although I generally like responding to critics and enjoy pitting my observations and evidence against theirs, somehow this seemed different.

The Game of Disrespect

Finally it occurred to me *why* this was different. The response of these so-called "educators" disrespected me ("your sales pitch"), disrespected my ideas ("silicon snake oil," "data without context"), and ultimately disrespected all the 21st century students about whom I was writing.

For the first time, I began to see just how much disrespect goes on between the generations, both in our classrooms and in our homes. If you ask most teachers (or parents), they'll probably swear up and down that they *do* respect their kids. But what do they say to them? One high school student reported to me that his parents told him, "Your computer games are a total waste of your time, money, and brain cells." Given that this student spends a lot of time playing these games, which are often more challenging than his schoolwork, and that he is proud of succeeding at them, this comment reflects *enormous* disrespect. The kid was pretty hurt by it.

But what goes around comes around. We all know how fluent parents and teachers are with today's digital technology—NOT!— and how easy it is for kids to master it. Digital technology may well be the literacy of the 21st century, and by that standard, most of today's teachers are illiterate. That's certainly how many students see their teachers—and they disrespect them for it. "Don't even try to keep up with technology," said a middle school girl recently to a group of teachers. "You'll only look stupid."

Amazingly, even parents and teachers get in on the disrespect game, one pitted against the other. "The cookies on my daughter's computer know more about her interests than her teachers do," quipped a well-known scientist recently. It's funny, yes, and has a grain of truth. But it's also disrespectful. And if we could hear the discussions taking place daily in teachers lounges, how much disrespect for students—and parents—might we find there? Having been there, I can tell you. Plenty.

Learners and Teachers

With such an atmosphere of mutual disrespect festering in our classrooms, learning is becoming increasingly difficult. Before you can teach or learn from someone, you need to genuinely respect them.

So how do we inject mutual respect—rather than mutual disrespect—into our classrooms? We must foster the important message that each of us, whether adult or kid, teacher or student, is every day a learner in some areas and a teacher in others.

Adults must accept that our kids have a lot to teach us, not only about technology, but also about 21st century life in general, and that we can and should learn from them every day. Kids need to understand, particularly in light of today's rapid technological advances, that their teachers have important lessons to teach *about* technology—such as the meaning of research and of truth in an era rife with data and technical manipulation.

Until we all "get it," I propose that we post in large letters in all of our classrooms—and above our bathroom mirrors, if need be—the following sign:

We Are All Learners. We Are All Teachers.

We should not only post this meaningful slogan but also reflect on it every day—alone and with our students—and contemplate its many meanings for what we are all struggling to do.

19

Let's Be "Digital Multipliers"

Eliminating the digital divide is something educators can and should do

Published in Educational Technology

When I speak to teachers I am almost always asked a question about equity, such as "My students don't all have the technology, and we don't have the money to provide it for every student, so what can I do?" Educators need to know that this very important question has an answer. I provide it in this essay.

☙ ☙ ❧ ❧

Whenever I speak to educators I typically get some variation of the "digital divide" question:

"I want to use technology, but my students don't all have equal access to it. Many (or some) don't have computers at home. Some (or many) don't own a cell phone. Some of their families can't afford monthly connection charges. By requiring they use this technology, am I not depriving these kids of an equal education?"

Clearly, the desire to not deprive any child of a good, and equal, education is laudable, and represents the best of intentions. But in some cases, our good intentions can lead us to behaviors that are not in the best interests of all our students.

An example of this is the following, which I once heard a teacher say. "Twenty-nine of my students have computers at home, but one doesn't. So I don't assign computer homework, because it wouldn't be fair to that student."

What about the other 29 students? Do we deprive 29 to be fair to one? Or do we find another solution for the one?

Whether our schools, or our students, can afford it or not, all of today's students need technology. Already, truck drivers have GPS, computers, and company-provided cell phones. Delivery people have handhelds. People in business are increasingly tethered to their BlackBerries. No matter how old-school one is in thinking that the tools of the past are sufficient for a good education, it does not take much foresight to realize that most work in the future will be technology-mediated.

I think we should scrounge, beg, borrow, and steal (figuratively) to get at least some technology to every student who doesn't have access to it, as quickly and as often as possible. But, of course, we can't just go out as individuals and buy the technology for those who don't have it. So what do we do to bridge, and eliminate, the digital divide in our schools and our students?

Accept Some Inequality

First, it's important to understand that not every student needs to have the same exact technology. Some think that school (or at least public school) should make sure every student has exactly the same things: the same pens, pencils or paper, the same textbooks, the same lunch, even, in some places, the same clothing (i.e., uniforms). We either provide all of these things to all students at public expense, or we don't use them. This may make sense for some things. But I don't think it makes sense for digital technology.

Digital technology access is unequal by its nature—or at least by the way we make and sell it—and always will be. We can set a floor—a set of minimum specifications—but some people will always want more. There is a huge variety of feature choices available, and each device is a set of tradeoffs, enabling every person to get the feature set he or she prefers and can afford. Few of us have the same phones, computers, stereos, speakers, etc., nor would we want to.

So the best solution may not be providing the same technology to every student, but rather finding accommodations for those who don't have their own. Increasingly, in the workplace, we see young workers wanting to use their own technology rather than what is provided. While getting cheaper (the $200 computer is here!) technology still costs money, which means that not everyone will get it in the same way, any more than everyone gets to work or is able to dress the same way. So perhaps we should not care exactly which technology our students use, and we should let the ones who have more use it. But we should make sure they are all using something.

So What Can We Do?

What we must be concerned about is students' wanting or needing access to a minimal level of digital technology and not being able to get it. If we, as educators, make it our business to see that every student has "enough" access, rather than "equal" access to digital technology, and is required to use their technology every day for difficult, stimulating, collaborative, world-involving projects, I think many, if not most of our "digital divide" issues will go away.

Here are some suggestions for accomplishing this *without* more money from the administration, and *without* spending money from our own pockets.

- First, let's be sure we use all the technology we do have at hand, and that it is the students who are using it. If there is an electronic whiteboard, the students should be using it to present, not the teacher. If some of our students have their own laptops or cell phones, let's make use of them.
- Next, let's maximize sharing. If not everyone in the class has a particular piece of technology, a teacher can put students into groups around a device, such as a computer or cell phone. The lesson/tasks can be structured in such a way that every student is required to use the device, with students teaching their peers and taking responsibility for all students knowing how to use the technology. Students can also share devices, keeping their own work on cheap USB drives.

- Then, let's increase access time. Places where all students can access technology, such as libraries and computer labs, should be kept open as long as possible—ideally every night until midnight—and on weekends. If transportation or safety is an issue, we can find volunteers to run carpools.
- Finally, let's do our best to get some technology for those who don't have access to it. Building one's own computer is inexpensive and easy, not to mention a great learning experience. Amazing bargains are available on eBay and other places online. Perfectly good cell phones and computers are thrown away and recycled regularly. With open source, Google Docs and shareware, software costs have dropped radically or disappeared. Plenty of individuals and foundations are willing to donate. Let's use our creativity to get hold of as much of this stuff as possible. And then let's use the students to maintain it and keep it useable.

If we (and our students) are willing to be creative, I see no reason why there should be a digital divide *at all* anywhere in the United States. As educators, we should take it as our responsibility to see that this no longer happens. It is easy to pass off eliminating the "digital divide" as someone else's responsibility, but it is really our own. This is a clear place where educators can be a big part of the solution—even without additional funding. I suggest we begin thinking of ourselves as "digital multipliers"—i.e., people who find creative solutions that bring every student, no matter what his or her background or income level, into the digital world—and get the job done.

Of course, there is also a second, more subtle, cause of the "digital divide." Certain educators, who are themselves afraid of the technology, are not making the best efforts they could to have all their students use technology as much as possible. Although this is often justified in "our kids don't need technology to think" language, it is really just another form of digital division and deprivation. It must be fought.

20

Search Versus Research

Or, the fear of Wikipedia overcome by new understanding for a digital era

The Internet in general, and Wikipedia in particular, pose a thorny problem for many educators: what and how to teach kids when all factual information is online, but its truth is rarely guaranteed by any formal authority such as an editor or publisher. Some schools and educators advocate banning students' use of the Internet and Wikipedia altogether. Others focus on specific ways to ascertain whether or not a site or information is trustworthy. I offer another approach: helping students distinguish between "search," where all is permissible, and "research," which has specific rules and requirements. I hope you, like many others, find this distinction helpful.

◌ ◌ ◌ ◌

We don't let our kids access Wikipedia.
We don't know if it's accurate.

—A school librarian

I shiver every time one of
my students cites Wikipedia in a paper.

—Danah Boyd

As soon as any new technology comes down the pike, be it TV, phones, cell phones, cameras, video cams, or the Wikipedia, the good old American school tradition is always ready . . .

. . . to fear and ban it!

Never mind that new technologies give our kids access to whole new worlds—they may not be worlds the teachers can control. Never mind that with cameras in their phones kids can collect and share visual data of all sorts, from their own faces to natural phenomena— someone might take a picture in the toilet. Never mind that kids have access to the Internet in their pockets—they might cheat. Never mind that we can finally, at no cost via webcams, share with parents, administrators, and the world what goes on in our classrooms— someone's privacy (particularly the teacher's!) might be invaded.

Others have written about how TV and land-line telephones were systematically excluded from American classrooms. For all the speed with which we've introduced computers for every student into our schools, we've effectively, up to this point, banned them as well. I've written elsewhere of the folly of banning cell phones from our kids' education (see "What Can You Learn From a Cell Phone? Almost Anything!" in this volume).

But the latest absurdity I've been hearing about is banning kids from citing—or even looking at—the Wikipedia—one of the most innovative and far-reaching products to come down the pike in a while—because it might not be as correct or accurate as a traditional encyclopedia written by paid experts.

If that's our criterion for what kids can read and cite, we'd better rethink kids' access to the Bible!

Ban or Teach?

Why is the rush always to fear and to ban rather than to teach?

If our kids use phones to take pictures in the bathrooms, it's our job to teach them the importance of privacy (perhaps while secretly applauding their sense of humor?).

If kids use cell phones to get information during tests, it's our job to teach them the importance of fairness (perhaps while secretly applauding their ingenuity!).

And if our kids use and cite only the Wikipedia, it's our job not to shiver but to help them learn to distinguish between "search" and "research" (perhaps while secretly recognizing our own intellectual lapses as well).

Search Versus Research

The tradition of search is a relatively new one—certainly less than a decade old. Hard as it is to believe, it has been only in the past couple of years that you can type whatever you are looking for into a little box and, wherever you happen to be, get all the information the world offers for free on that subject. The quantity of information is unbelievable. However, the *quality* of that information is, in most cases, not particularly well indicated.

Which is why we have "research"—a whole different animal from "search."

The tradition of research, in a school or academic setting, is a long and important one, and was established precisely for the purpose of determining the quality of information. The research tradition encompasses why and how we cite our sources, what sources are considered "primary" versus "secondary," what types and sources of information are considered more reliable, trustworthy, or accurate, and many other things.

If our students don't know or understand these differences, it's our job as educators to make sure they do. Kids need to know that while search involves just looking, research involves a whole discipline of behaviors. (What those behaviors are, if you don't already know, can be found easily via search ☺.)

So far so good. However . . .

Assuming we ever did, we no longer live in clear-cut times. We live, rather, in blurry, super-fast-changing times. One of the most important things for all of us, young and old, to learn and do in these times and circumstances is to figure out how to continually adapt our ideas (and get used to the idea of adapting them)—even those that have long traditions behind them—to new conditions and technologies that emerge. The Wikipedia is only the first of a great many changes to come. But it's a good place to start thinking differently.

What Is Wikipedia?

So what is Wikipedia, and what's the "story" behind it? If you're not aware, Wikipedia is a new beast in the world, born in 2001. To a searcher, it acts exactly like an online encyclopedia. You type www.wikipedia.org into your browser, enter a topic, and get back an "article" about that topic (if one exists), precisely as in a traditional encyclopedia like the *Britannica Online*. What differentiates Wikipedia from the traditional encyclopedia it is that its articles are not written by hired "experts" (the *Britannica* uses more than 4,000 of them), but by anyone who chooses to write or contribute. Here's the Wikipedia entry on "Wikipedia" (pronounced as either "week-ee-peedia" or "wick-ee-peedia"): "Wikipedia is a multilingual, web-based, free-content encyclopedia . . . written collaboratively by volunteers. . . ." The writers use wiki software, meaning articles can be added or changed by nearly anyone. The project began on January 15, 2001, as a complement to the expert-written Nupedia and is now operated by the nonprofit Wikimedia Foundation. It has steadily risen in popularity and spawned several sister projects, such as Wiktionary, Wikibooks, and Wikinews.

Articles in Wikipedia are regularly cited by the mass media and academia, who praise it for its free distribution, editing, and diverse range of coverage. Editors are encouraged to uphold a policy of "neutral point of view," under which notable perspectives are summarized without an attempt to determine an objective truth. Yet due to its open nature, vandalism and inaccuracy are continual problems—and the status of Wikipedia as reference work has been controversial. It has also been criticized for systemic bias, preference of consensus to credentials, and a perceived lack of accountability and authority when compared with traditional encyclopedias.

There are about 200 language editions of Wikipedia (about 100 of which are active). Ten editions—English, German, French, Japanese, Italian, Polish, Swedish, Dutch, Portuguese, and Spanish—have more than 50,000 articles each. Its German-language edition has been distributed on compact discs, and many of its other editions are mirrored or have been forked (see http://en.wikipedia.org/wiki/Fork_%28software%29) by websites.

So with more than 50,000 articles and 200 languages, you can see this is no small thing. No article on the topic you are searching for? Create your own! All Wikipedia articles begin with a single contribution by a single person, who thinks he or she has some knowledge of some topic (which the writer picks and names) and who is motivated to contribute. Some topics never go beyond this one contribution.

But the power of the wiki technology that lies behind the Wikipedia is that literally anybody who wants to can change or add to that original article, merely by hitting the Edit button. In other words, on a wiki, everyone's an editor. And this is what makes it, in its own words, "controversial."

For topics of wide interest, many people (tens, hundreds, or even thousands) are motivated to read, contribute, and change the entry and often do so on a regular basis. Many argue that this process effectively culls out mistakes and makes many articles just as (or, some might say, even more) reliable—and almost certainly more up to date—than their counterparts in the *Britannica* or its brethren. (Whether this is in fact true, and how one might go about determining whether it is true, is a great topic for a class discussion.) The history of the changes to each article is also there for all to see.

It is fascinating to see how quickly a Wikipedia article emerges on a contemporary topic, such as Hurricane Katrina, often while the event is still happening. Someone writes a few lines, others add, and suddenly there are pages, pictures, and more.

So, one beginning lesson for students using Wikipedia is to look at the number of changes and additions to an article and the number of authors. More may mean more reliable information.

But of course it's not that simple. Because information contains points of view. Was the Battle of Gettysburg a great, nation-saving event, a humiliating defeat, or just a bloody massacre? Was the 2005 war in Iraq an attempt to liberate a people, an attempt to further a political system, or a thinly disguised protection of American oil interests? Were Pearl Harbor and 9/11 vile sneak attacks or brilliant military maneuvers? Is evolution "the" answer or "an" answer?

To address this, the Wikipedia, as noted, has established a "neutral point of view" policy, asking that all points of view be included and all sides of an issue discussed. This is not always easy, but it may include more information than an article by an expert, whose point of view might not be so obvious. (Again, a good topic for class discussion: Review some traditional encyclopedia articles on the topics mentioned. Are all points of view represented?)

So, other than to count the number of authors in an article, what *should* we teach our kids about Wikipedia?

First, that it's a source. Second, that it's *never* the only source.

And third, that merely searching, finding, and citing the Wikipedia—or even the *Britannica*—does not constitute research, even by an elementary school kid. Students need to be taught early to cross-check information, to consult multiple sources, and to go to, read, and cite original documents and sources when they exist. Especially in this time and political climate, students must be taught not to necessarily believe what they hear or read—even from so-called experts—but to always look for additional, corroborating sources. (By the way, that's the *re* in *research*.)

A Hypothetical Example

And we should start inculcating good habits early. To me a gem of a third grade (or so) research paper might read something like this:

Abraham Lincoln

By . . .

(Source of image: www.historyplace.com)

My Google search on "Abraham Lincoln" returned 10 million hits. According to all the sources I consulted (listed at the end), Abraham Lincoln was President of the United States from 1861 to 1865. The *Wikipedia* calls Abraham Lincoln one of our greatest presidents. So does the *Encyclopedia Britannica* and so do several of his biographies I consulted. I therefore conclude that he was one of our greatest presidents. A timeline of Abraham Lincoln's life was found by me online at http://www.historyplace.com/lincoln/#prez on October 13, 2005. Some highlights include . . .

All my sources agree that Lincoln freed the slaves in 1862 with the Emancipation Proclamation. That document reads, in part, "all persons held as slaves within any State or designated part of a State, the people whereof shall then be in rebellion against the United States, shall be then, thenceforward, and forever, free." To me, this means that . . .

New Understanding: How to Help Our Students in a Digital Era

Fellow teachers, librarians, and parents, let us all be clear. Our kids will always find and use whatever new thing appears. We oughtn't *ban* the Wikipedia, or *any* new technology, ever. Nor should we fear these technologies.

As educators our duty is to *teach* our students to understand both the power and the limitations of all the new technological tools that are, and will increasingly be, at our kids' disposal. It is our job to show them how they can use all these new tools well and wisely.

Of course the first step in doing this is to understand the tools ourselves. So on what topic will *you* be writing *your* first Wikipedia article?

21

Simulation Nation

Inventive computer sims can turn dull lessons into hyperreal experiences—if we can get educators to use them

Published in Edutopia

Most of my essays arise naturally from my experiences and observations. This essay, however, was "commissioned"—that is, I didn't decide to write it on my own but was asked to write it by an editor. I tried, though, to put a different "spin" on it from the usual commissioned piece about a particular technology.

ଔ ଔ ဢ ဢ

Articles in the media on the use of some particular technology in schools are generally pretty formulaic. Typically, they begin with a glowing quote from a teacher, who bubbles, "I use [insert technology] with my classes, and it's the greatest thing since sliced pasta."

Then they throw in a few case studies, ideally from different parts of the world and various types of schools (say, urban and rural) for the requisite diversity. Toss in a few more highly enthusiastic instructors and a ringing endorsement from a student, and—boom—you're home free. "I should look into that," thinks you, dear reader.

If that's the kind of article you are looking for, keep looking, because this [essay] on computer-simulation technology is, rather, about how and why yet another technology that could be enormously powerful for our kids' learning is getting short shrift in our educational system—despite the successes we can, in fact, find and cite. Simulation is not just another in the long line of passing fads (or short-term opportunities) in educational technology. It is, rather, a real key to helping our students understand the world.

Computer-simulation technology is a way of looking at objects or systems that encourage a learner not only to wonder, "What would happen if . . . ?" but also to try out those alternatives virtually and see the consequences. It is a way for learners to acquire experience about how things and systems in the world behave, without actually touching them. I call it interactive pretending.

Because so many of the things we need to understand these days are either too complex, too vast, too small, too far, or too dangerous to be experienced directly, we can no longer rely, as we did for so long, on hands-on learning. Simulation provides us a solution and is, in fact, the only way to experience, try, and learn many of things we really want to know about (and want our students to learn about). Because of this factor, simulation is absolutely fundamental to education—and has always been so.

Several principles are key for educators to understand.

Simulation is not new. It has been with us for as long as there has been education. At its core, simulation requires no other technology than the ability to think. Most simulations take place entirely in the mind, via mental what-ifs: A lawyer plays through an upcoming trial in his head. A skier visualizes herself slaloming down the course. Our best teachers have always used mental simulations with their students, as when they announce, "What if the South had won the Civil War?" or "Imagine if penicillin was never invented." It requires nothing more than a teacher who can think through the possibilities with students and help them envisage possible consequences and outcomes. Computers help by overlaying a lot of the details, but simulation always comes back to a person asking, "What if?"

Simulation helps us understand complex issues. This is particularly true of complicated computer model simulation. Today, we can model amazingly complex behaviors while providing relatively simple inputs and clear sensual outputs. With these simulations, students learn about a complicated thing (say, an airplane), system (the weather), or behavior (management), and, without risk of damaging anything or getting hurt themselves, make a wide variety of assumptions and changes and see the results.

Simulation is real-world experience. Professional simulations are used every day in just about every profession: City planners simulate all the factors that make a metropolis thrive or die. Military planners simulate conditions, battles, and equipment. Traders simulate financial markets. Weather forecasters simulate daily and long-term climate. Doctors simulate the effects of drugs, transplants, and other interventions. Ecologists simulate changes in the environment. Engineers simulate the effects of natural and artificial forces on buildings and bridges. Computer-network engineers simulate conditions on the Internet. Scientists use simulations continually.

How Do We Know They Work?

OK, you're convinced. But how do you get the school board (or even your own principal) to back you? Proving the effectiveness of any given teaching technique for learning is a task fraught with problems, if not downright impossible. The trouble is that keeping constant everything else besides the teaching technique in question (the students, the time, the material, and so on) is untenable. In addition, students may learn different things from various techniques—some of which, although valuable, are not measured by our usual evaluations.

But for those who can be satisfied with real-world acceptance, rather than pseudoscientific studies, we have lots of empirical evidence that people learn from simulation, and that simulations therefore have great teaching value.

NASA's astronaut training puts learners through simulated events. Airlines have pilots go directly from the simulator to the yoke of a 747. Medical students learn the physical relationships of body parts and how systems work together. They have progressed from learning on cadavers to working with physical simulators and, more recently, onscreen simulators. If a prospective doctor can learn about a complex piece of anatomy or a difficult procedure from a simulator, certainly our kids can learn the frog's interior layout from a sim like Froguts.

The corporate world provides useful data about simulations designed to change behavior and obtain results (which is exactly what we hope will be learned in many situations but is something that few, if any, of our standardized achievement tests measure). In one comparison of learning certain management techniques, performance of teams led by people who had learned through a simulation called Virtual Leader, by Simulearn, beat the teams whose managers had learned via the standard method (coaching) by a margin of 22 percent.

All the above evidence, of course, overlaps.

So, giving our kids a simulation of, say, a piston engine and expecting them to understand how the engine works and then fix the engine in reality is not only realistic but also in line with what occurs in the best of our business communities.

The Sad State of Sims in Schools

Given that simulation (1) is an important key to producing learning and understanding, (2) will play a big part of the student's professional life, and (3) is a teaching tool that demonstrably works, it certainly makes sense to ask the question "What is the state of simulation in our K–12 schools?"

Sadly, the use of simulation in elementary schools and secondary schools is far more infrequent and unorganized than it could, and should, be. Why? The reason we don't see more simulation used in K–12 classrooms is not that lots of good educational simulations don't exist. Nor is it the case that teachers aren't using simulation; some do.

But not nearly enough. Although it's impossible to tell precisely how much simulation is used, I began my research by asking people I thought would be the most likely to know—professors in forward-thinking education schools, and experts in corporate simulations. After much thinking and searching, they collectively came up with exactly one teacher and a couple graduate students. Makers of simulation software, of course—especially the software that is for sale—do have their customers. And I hope that any teacher using simulations who reads this [essay] will write to me and volunteer to become part of a database of teachers willing to share their own experiments and successes.

But of our 2.2 million teachers, I would be shocked to learn that even 1 percent use simulations in class. I'd be surprised if it were even one-tenth of that. It's probably more like one one-hundredth. (Please, folks, write in and prove me wrong.)

It is my strong sense that in America's K–12 educational system, simulations are being used only in isolated and nonsystematic ways compared to other teaching tools such as textbooks, videos, and traditional science manipulatives. This meager usage is detrimental to the education of our 21st century kids, and must change.

Barriers

Why aren't simulations more widely used in our schools? Let's take a look.

Lack of Money. Cost is often cited as an issue, although it shouldn't be. School simulations either are, or are headed toward, being free. This is how it should be: If education is a public good, its tools should be freely available to all teachers and students. Sites such as Froguts, which started as a site with free registration, attracted a large number of teachers, and then began to charge, are, I think, a poor model. Even with relatively modest prices, they become unaffordable to, and unusable by, many.

As more and more free Internet simulations become available, providing similar offerings, those trying to make money by selling their simulations to schools, parents, or teachers are destined to change their policies or be left behind. Unfortunately, we lack business models that will allow creators to earn a living while letting public school students use their simulations at no charge. We need to find more.

Lack of Time. As long as we have extensive curricula teachers feel they need to cover by lecturing, time will be a barrier. There simply isn't adequate time in the school year to present everything, much less use alternative learning tools such as simulation. The significance attached to testing, which often causes everything in the class schedule that does not directly apply to the test to be eliminated, exacerbates this condition.

In addition, educators generally are not good at using simulations as part of curricular learning, or at including in our standardized testing the lessons simulations teach. Traditionalist instructors who want to keep teaching the old hands-on way oppose attempts to replace traditional labs with simulations (at much lower cost). These teachers need to be reminded that simulation is how today's real scientists actually work and how many other professionals actually learn their job skills, whether manual, mental, or managerial.

Lack of Knowledge. Many teachers have never experienced simulation as learners and are unaware of its power and importance. A large number began their careers when the ability to simulate through computers did not exist. Some still think "simulation" is accomplished just by playing a video in class. They need to be taught that, though showing students a movie or an animation of something happening can be more instructive than just reading about it, true simulation (which is even more instructive) means that students can change variables and affect the outcome. As for teachers who say, "I don't know how to find simulations in my field," a Google search on "teachers simulation school" will call up plenty.

Lack of Technology. The best technology-based simulations available do require relatively modern computers or handhelds, and often global-positioning-system technology and broadband connections as well, which not all schools have. Therefore, extra creativity is often required to figure out ways to use these simulations—say, for example, as homework or computer-lab work. And let's not forget the many non-computer-based simulations available.

Lack of Sharing. In the age of the Internet, it seems logical that when something works for a teacher in one classroom, it should be quickly broadcast to everyone teaching that class or level. But our teachers, for the most part, are terrible at sharing. Those who have success with simulations owe it to their colleagues to post what they do on the Web—as an HTML page, a Web site, a blog entry, or a video— available for all to see.

Bust the Barriers

How do we eliminate the barriers?

Think of simulation as a free resource. Between noncomputer simulations and free simulations on the Internet, plenty are available. Help the creators of sites that charge understand that taxpayer money or philanthropy—not teachers or parents—should pay for school supplies and that they should find a better funding model than bait-and-switch (offer it free, hook teachers, and then charge them for it).

Use simulation not to invade teaching time but to make better use of it. Investigate whether particular simulations can replace some lessons or lectures. Assign online simulations to groups to try at home, in a lab, or an after-school program. Replace live lab time with computer simulation.

When technology is unavailable, try noncomputer simulations— either ones that exist or thought experiments you and your students invent.

Educate yourself. An evening's exploration using Google and the links in this article will expand your horizons immensely. Find out what others are doing in your subject area. Assuming they are willing to offer their information (and I hope they are), we will share with you the names of all the teachers who write in to say they are using simulation. And don't be afraid to ask your students what simulations they like and use on their own.

Realize that you need not abandon preparation for standardized tests to conduct simulations; the exams can be simulated as well. A discussion of how to do this would be well worth some class time. (Hint: A review test is a simulation. Now ask, "What if . . . ?")

Finally, despite the disclaimer at the beginning of this article, endorsements from teachers are always useful, and you can find a number on the Internet.

The value of simulation is that it can, paradoxically, bring more reality into your students' learning, and it can do this for just about any subject or subject matter. As with all educational technologies, your two biggest resources for using it well (essentially the only ones that matter) are your peers and your students. Make good use of them both.

22

What Can You Learn From a Cell Phone? Almost Anything!

Published in Innovate

I am particularly proud of this essay, because it kick-started a movement where none existed before: incorporating students' own digital tools, particularly their phones, into their education. For a long time this was anathema to educators, and in some places still is (although attitudes here are quickly changing). When Liz Kolb, creator of Toys to Tools *(a blog and book about using cell phones in class) first went looking for information about doing so, this essay, she told me, was the only thing she found. Now there are several books available in addition to hers. In fact, as the editor of this volume pointed out, most of the works cited in this essay are old and the information is no longer current, but many of the predictions have come true. For example, the introduction of "app phones" has made cell phones even more useful for learning, although even the basic voice and text functions of all cell phones can still be used as important learning tools. As more teachers realize this and more students begin using their phones—either with permission or stealthily—more and more useful ways to use these important learning tools will come to light. I hope that all teachers will share their own successes and learn—primarily through short videos—to make full use of these rapidly growing ways of increasing our students' learning.*

ʕʕ ʕʕ ʒɔ ʒɔ

One and a half billion people, all over the world, are walking around with powerful computers in their pockets and purses. The fact is they often do not realize it, because they call them something else. But today's high-end cell phones have the computing power of a mid-1990s personal computer (PC)—while consuming only one one-hundredth of the energy. Even the simplest, voice-only phones have more complex and powerful chips than the 1969 onboard computer that landed a spaceship on the moon.

In the United States, it is almost universally acknowledged that computers are essential for 21st century students. To most educators "computer" means a PC, a laptop, or, in some instances, a personal digital assistant (PDA); cell phones, on the other hand, are more often regarded as bothersome distractions to the learning process. However, it is time to begin thinking of our cell phones as computers—even more powerful in some ways than their bigger cousins. Both have microchips and perform logical functions. The main difference is that the phones began with, and still have, small size, radio transmission, and communication as their core features, expanding out toward calculation and other functions. This has happened at precisely the same time as the calculation machines we call computers have expanded into communication and other areas. Clearly the two are headed toward meeting in the middle; when all the miniaturization problems have been solved, the result will be tiny, fully featured devices that we carry around (or perhaps have implanted in our bodies).

For now, most educators still see the computer and the cell phone as very different devices, with the tiny cell phone being a much more personal (and ubiquitous) accoutrement, especially among young people. In the United States, the penetration of student mobile phones is 40 percent in many junior high schools and 75 percent in many high schools (NOP World 2005); according to a Student Monitor survey (as cited in Kinzie 2005), penetration is 90 percent in U.S. colleges. With dropping prices and increasing utility, it is almost a foregone conclusion that not too far into the future, *all* students will have a cell phone, quite possibly built right into their clothing. Ski parkas with built-in cell phones are already on the market. Yet Americans do not fully appreciate the potential of these devices; from a cell phone perspective, we remain PC-centric laggards.

Meanwhile, the cell phone—generally called a mobile phone outside of the United States—has proved so useful elsewhere that there are 1.5 billion around the world, with half a billion new ones sold every year (Stone 2004). The country where the computer was invented, along with its northern neighbor, Canada, are the only places where PCs still outnumber cell phones. In the rest of the world the mobile reigns, with countries often having 5 to 10 times more mobile phones than PCs.

In some countries—including the United Kingdom, Italy, Sweden, and Czechoslovakia—cell phone penetration is *greater than* 100 percent, which means that individuals own and use two or more of these devices (Borghese 2005; Agence France-Presse 2005). Cell phone penetration in Asia continues to climb: Hong Kong and Taiwan have already surpassed 100 percent according to one prominent survey (IT Facts 2004; Simon 2004), and several years ago, *J@pan Inc* magazine reported that more than 90 percent of Tokyo high schoolers carried mobile phones (2001). Usage is increasing wildly across the globe, notably where relatively inexpensive cell systems bring service to areas without land lines. In Botswana, roughly one of every four citizens owned a mobile phone by 2002 (Central Intelligence Agency 2005, "People"; "Communications"). Moreover, students in China, the Philippines, and Germany are using their mobile phones to learn English; to study math, health, and spelling; and to access live and archived university lectures, respectively (BBC Press Office 2005; Villafania 2004; Chapman 2003).

Cell phones are not just communications devices sparking new modalities of interaction between people; they are also particularly useful computers that fit in your pocket, are always with you, and are nearly always on. Like all communication and computing devices, cell phones can be used to learn. So rather than fight the trend of kids coming to school carrying their own powerful learning devices—which they have already paid for—why not use the opportunity to their educational advantage?

Designing Cell Phones as Learning Tools

Can cell phones really provide their owners with the knowledge, skills, behaviors, and attitudes that will help them succeed in their schools, their jobs, and their lives? I maintain that the only correct answer to the question of what students can learn with a cell phone is "*anything,* if we educators design it right." There are many different kinds of learning and many processes that people use to learn, but among the most frequent, time-tested, and effective of these are listening, observing, imitating, questioning, reflecting, trying, estimating, predicting, speculating, and practicing. *All* of these learning processes can be supported through cell phones. In addition, cell phones complement the short-burst, casual, multitasking style of today's "Digital Native" learners. Using cell phones as learning devices, whether in or out of school, requires a good deal of rethinking and flexibility on the part of educators. Yet given the opportunity, students will quickly embrace, use, and make the tool their own in various unexpected ways—just as they have been doing with all useful digital technology.

Feature Segmentation

So what and how can our students—including adult trainees—learn from their cell phones?

A useful way to answer this question is to consider the capabilities that phones in use today possess, and to see what each capability brings us. With half a billion cell phones sold each year, the devices are hotbeds of feature innovation—the major features being voice, short messaging service (SMS), graphics, user-controlled operating systems, downloadables, browsers, camera functions (still and video), and geopositioning—with new features such as fingerprint readers, sensors, and voice recognition being added every day. In addition, optional hardware and software accessories are available as both input mechanisms (e.g., thumb keyboards and styli) and optional output systems (e.g., plug-in screens and headphones).

Voice Only

The most basic phones—those with voice capabilities only—are still the most prevalent in the world, although they are fast being replaced and upgraded. They are basically radios that pick up and send signals on certain predetermined frequencies.

Is there anything students can learn on a voice-only phone? Languages, literature, public speaking, writing, storytelling, and history are just a few of the subjects that are highly adaptable to voice-only technology. Of these, language is probably the most obvious. Given the huge demand and market around the world for English lessons and practice, it is the one kind of learning that is already readily available on cell phones. In Japan, you can dial a number on your cell for short English lessons from ALC Press's Pocket Eijiro (McNicol 2004) or Japanese lessons from Enfour's TangoTown. In China, the British Broadcasting Corporation (BBC) and others are providing cell phone English-language training (BBC Press Office 2005). One company, MIG China Ltd. (working with First International Digital), is even subtitling pop songs with their lyrics, highlighting each word as it is sung (First International Digital 2004). Companies such as Ectaco provide language games via mobile phone "flash cards," as well as dictionary and phrase book software to aid in foreign language proficiency. And the Canadian corporation Go Test Go has developed English vocabulary testing software. While many of these sites have quickly moved to the mixed media that the phones in their regions support, much of what they offer can be made available easily on voice-only phones. Creating an interactive voice-only cell phone learning application today requires no more than the simple technology used to direct help desk callers, development kits for which are available for under $500.

Other types of voice-only learning applications exist and are growing in popularity. In Concord, Massachusetts, you can use a cell phone for guided tours of Minute Man National Historical Park, where the "shot heard 'round the world" was fired. As part of Ultralab's eVIVA project, Anglia Polytechnic University (in the United Kingdom) has experimented successfully with using cell phones for exams, with the students' voice prints authenticating that they are the ones being tested (*BBC News* 2003; McGuire, Roberts, and Moss 2004). And it doesn't have to stop there. Have you ever listened to *Car Talk* or *Fresh Air* on NPR, or to the BBC? Remember, cell phones are basically radios. Students don't need anything more than a voice link and a person on the other end worth listening to in order to learn a great deal. Why not offer cell-phone-delivered lectures (really engaging ones) on basic subjects, with cell phone call-ins and multiway discussions?

An immediate advantage of voice-only learning is that we know it works—for millennia it was the only type of learning humans had. While some "Digital Immigrant" adults may have a difficult time with, and even question the value of, non-face-to-face voice communication for learning, virtual relationships are now second nature to students, and often preferred.

Short Text Messages

SMS, only recently introduced in the United States, has been available on cell phones outside the country for several years. This feature has spread like wildfire among young people in Europe and Asia, with literally billions of SMS messages being sent every day around the world. Short text messages, which can be written quickly, even in your pocket (especially with predictive text), offer enormous learning opportunities.

Currently, SMS messages provide timely "learning" reminders and encouragement for people trying to change their behavior (e.g., for someone who wants to quit smoking). SMS is also the technology used for voting on the television show *American Idol*. Marketers use SMS for informational quizzes about subjects of interest to young people, such as movie and television stars. And innovative SMS games, many of which have strong educational potential, are attracting large playing audiences. (For more information on recent developments in SMS technology, see the textually.org weblog.)

In schools, SMS can be used to conduct pop quizzes or spelling or math tests, to poll students' opinions, to make learners aware of current events for class discussion (e.g., with messages from Cable News Network's *Breaking News*), and even to tutor students. Outside of school, test preparation companies such as The Princeton Review, Kaplan, and Go Test Go are already offering cell-phone-delivered test-preparation questions (for the Scholastic Achievement Test and others) at specific user-preferred times. Educators easily could use SMS technology to provide cell phone learners, individually and in competitive or collaborative groups, with data and clues in real time for analysis, diagnosis, and response, whether in a historical, literary, political, scientific, medical, or machine-maintenance context.

Graphic Displays

Just about every cell phone has some kind of graphic display, even if it shows only the signal and battery strength and the name and/or number of a contact. Most new cell phones come with far more graphic power than that—they typically sport bright color screens that can crisply display words, pictures, and animation. Many of these screens have resolutions of 320×240 pixels—half the screen size of the standard computer of not too long ago—and higher. They present thousands of colors and even three-dimensional images and holograms.

Such high-resolution screens allow for meaningful amounts of text to be displayed, either paragraph by paragraph or one quickly flashed word at a time, known as RSVP—rapid serial visual presentation—with the user setting (and generally greatly increasing) his or her own reading speed. A service called BuddyBuzz offers content from Reuters and CNet using RSVP. In Asia, novels intended to be read on phone screens are already being written (Web Japan 2004). Why not learning texts?

Better graphic displays also mean that text can be accompanied by pictures and animation (and, of course, sound—it *is* a phone). Many schools are currently using computers and handheld devices for animations in subjects such as anatomy and forensics; Bryan Edwards Publishing is one company that provides PDA-compatible animations to educational institutions. Cell phones can replace these handheld devices, especially given that many of the animations are in Flash, which currently runs on many cell phones and eventually will run on all of them. Macromedia already offers what it calls "Flash Lite" applications, including one for learning sign language. The Chemical Abstracts Service is preparing a database of molecule images that can be accessed via cell phone.

Japanese students have long learned everything from business to cooking through "manga," graphic novels that are now becoming popular in the West as well. At a recent computer show, a Japanese company handed out a manga pamphlet (about its "middleware" software) that could easily be displayed one frame at a time on a cell phone—similar to the so-called "mobile manga" that has recently become a phenomenon in Japan (Raugust 2004). It follows that in many cases, our mobile phones will be able to replace our textbooks, with the limited screen size of the phones being, in fact, a positive constraint that forces publishers to rethink their design and logic for maximum effectiveness, rather than just add pages.

Downloadable Programs

Now that cell phones have memories (or memory card slots) that accept downloaded programs and content, entire new learning worlds have opened up. Cell phone users can access versions of the same kinds of tools and teaching programs available on personal computers, and, given that the phones are communications devices, use the tools for collaboration in new and interesting ways. All manner of applications combining elements of voice, text, graphics, and even specially designed spreadsheets and word processors can be downloaded to phones, with additional content added as needed. Other tools currently available for download include browsers, fax senders, programming languages, and even an application that gives you access to your desktop computer.

Do you need to learn or review a particular subject? Do you want to practice for a professional school entrance exam? Soon you'll just download a program to your cell phone, text your friends, and start studying.

Internet Browsers

Internet browsers are now being built into a growing number of cell phones, especially those that use the faster third-generation protocol (3G). Sites and options designed specifically for Web-enabled cell phones are becoming more and more numerous. Having a browser in the cell phone puts a dictionary, thesaurus, and encyclopedia into the hands of every student. It gives them instant access to Google and other text search engines, turning their cell phones into research tools. For example, students studying nature, architecture, art, or design can search for images on the Web that match what they find in life in order to understand their properties, style, and form.

Cameras and Video Clips

Worldwide, 178 million camera phones were sold in 2004 (InfoTrends/CAP Ventures 2005), and in many places such phones are already accepted as the norm. Educationally—once students learn that privacy concerns are as important here as anywhere else—they are a gold mine. In class, cell phones with cameras provide possible tools for scientific data collection, documentation, and visual journalism, allowing students to gather evidence, collect and classify images, and follow progressions over time. Creative cell phone photos can inspire students' creative writing via caption or story contests. Phones can be placed in various (appropriate) places and operated remotely, allowing observations that would be impossible in person. Students can literally see what is going on around the world, including, potentially, learning activities in the classrooms of other countries.

Moreover, the first video cam phones are now hitting the market. They are capable of taking and sending short (typically 10- to 30-second) video clips. This feature extends the phone's learning possibilities even farther, into television journalism (most TV news clips are less than 30 seconds) as well as creative movie-making. A terrific educational use of short video clips would be modeling effective and ineffective behaviors relating to ethics, negotiation, and other subjects.

Global Positioning Systems (GPS)

The initial crude ability of cell phones to "know where they are" quickly became the basis of some very innovative applications, including mobile-phone-based multiplayer search games (more than a dozen are currently in circulation). Now sophisticated GPS satellite receivers that can pinpoint a phone's location to within a few feet are being built into many cell phones (and made available as add-ons for many others).

This feature allows cell phone learning to be location-specific. Students' cell phones can provide them with information about wherever they happen to be—in a city, in the countryside, or on a campus. So-called "augmented reality tours" have been designed (for example, see Papageorgiou et al. 2000), and someday most schools and colleges will use similar programs for orientation. The ability of students to determine their precise position has clear applications in geography, orienteering, archeology, architecture, science, and math, to name only a few subjects. Students can use cell phones with GPS to search for things and places (already known as "geocaching") or to pinpoint environmental dangers, as in the case of Environmental Detectives, a learning game from the Massachusetts Institute of Technology.

Reorienting Research and Practice

In Japan, Masayasu Morita, working with ALC Press, evaluated the use of English language lessons formatted differently for computers and cell phones. He found that 90 percent of cell phone users were still accessing the lessons after 15 days, compared to only 50 percent of computer users (2003). Another Japanese company, Cerego, strongly supports using cell phones for learning. Outside of Asia, however, I have found that the number of people learning with cell phones or doing research on cell-phone-based learning is exceedingly small.

Researchers such as Cathleen Norris and Elliot Soloway (2003) in the United States, Jill Attewell and Carol Savill-Smith (2004) in Great Britain, and Giorgio da Bormida and Paul Lefrere (2003) in Europe are experimenting with mobile devices for learning—but they typically use PDAs, not cell phones. The former are often donated by manufacturers eager to find a new market for their devices.

This is not the same as using *cell phones* for learning. There are fewer than 50 million PDAs in the world but more than 1.5 billion cell phones. Of course PDA-based research will be useful, but we will not be on the right track until educators begin thinking of using the computing and communication device *currently in the students' pockets* to support learning.

New Approaches and Emerging Ethics

As usual, students are far ahead of their teachers on this. The first educational use they have found (in large numbers) for their cell phones is retrieving information on demand during exams. Educators, of course, refer to this as "cheating." They might better serve their students by redefining open-book testing as open-phone testing, for example, and by encouraging, rather than quashing, student innovation in this and other areas. Let me state definitively that I am not in favor of cheating. I *am* in favor of adjusting the rules of test-taking and other educational practices in a way that fosters student ingenuity and creativity in using learning tools and that supports learning rather than administration.

As these sorts of adjustments happen, new norms and ethics will have to emerge around technology in classrooms. But existing norms can change quickly when a new one is better. Some people can remember how rapidly, in the 1970s, the norm went from "It's rude to have an answering machine" to "It's rude *not* to have an answering machine."

Educators should bear in mind that cell phones can be used for context as well as content (as in the aforementioned tour of Minute Man National Historical Park in Massachusetts). Those concerned that students use their tools not only to retrieve information but also to filter and understand it are the very people who should be figuring out how cell phones can meet this goal. Just as we are designing and refining Web- and PC-based tools for such tasks, so must we design similar tools for cell phones; the resulting communication and social features of the phones are likely to be of great help educationally.

Fully featured as cell phones are, it has been pointed out that they are not powerful enough to be students' *only* learning tool. This is, of course, true—and students will no doubt use whatever tools do the job, provided that they work well together. Cell phones can be our students' interface to a variety of computing devices, just as they control their entertainment devices. Even if future cell phone technology does not lend itself to every learning task, it will be suited to a wide range of tasks—and there is no reason not to take advantages of those capabilities.

Although I have tried to provide a variety of suggestions and examples of how cell phones might be used for learning, my goal here is not to present a complete vision, but rather to open the eyes of those who are ignoring an important resource for learning that is real and untapped today. I am convinced that once cell-phone-based learning is under way, the "world mind" of both educators and students will take it in a million useful and unexpected directions.

The Future

Cell phones are getting smaller and more powerful each day. The disposable cell phone is already patented and being manufactured; it is a mere two by three inches, with the thickness of three credit cards, and is made entirely of paper (the circuit board is printed with metallic conductive ink). Such phones, in volume, will likely cost less than a dollar each, with the air time for educational uses likely subsidized by carriers and others. Some already see mobile bills shrinking to only a few dollars as the mobile companies pay off their investments in the new networks (Stone 2004).

Although we often hear complaints from older Digital Immigrants about cell phones' limited screen and button size, it is precisely the combination of miniaturization, mobility, and power that grabs today's Digital Natives. They can visualize a small screen as a window to an infinite space and have quickly trained themselves to keyboard with their thumbs.

Despite what some may consider cell phones' limitations, our students are already inventing ways to use their phones to learn what *they* want to know. If educators are smart, we will figure out how to deliver *our* product in a way that fits into our students' digital lives— and their cell phones. Instead of wasting our energy fighting their preferred delivery system, we will be working to ensure that our students extract maximum understanding and benefit from the vast amounts of cell-phone-based learning of which they will, no doubt, soon take advantage.

References

Agence France-Presse. 2005. Czech mobile phone penetration exceeds 100 percent in 2004. *Technology.Designerz.com*, January 19. http://technology .news.designerz.com/czech-mobile-phone-penetration-exceeds -100-percent-in-2004.html (accessed June 1, 2005).

Attewell, J., and C. Savill-Smith, eds. 2004. *Learning with mobile devices: Research and development.* London: Learning and Skills Development Agency. http://www.lsda.org.uk/files/pdf/1440.pdf (accessed June 1, 2005).

BBC News. 2003. Testing students by mobile phone. November 17. http:// news.bbc.co.uk/1/hi/education/3278625.stm (accessed June 1, 2005).

BBC Press Office. 2005. BBC launches English University Tour in China. March 30. http://www.bbc.co.uk/pressoffice/pressreleases/stories/2005/03_march/30/china.shtml (accessed June 1, 2005).

Borghese, M. 2005. Western Europe to be over 100% mobile by 2007. *All Headline News,* April 6. http://www.allheadlinenews.com/articles/2230775906 (accessed June 1, 2005).

Central Intelligence Agency. 2005. The world factbook: Botswana. http://www.cia.gov/cia/publications/factbook/geos/bc.html (accessed June 1, 2005).

Chapman, C. 2003. German students to learn by phone. *The Times Higher Education Supplement,* July 11. http://www.thes.co.uk/search/story.aspx?story_id=93337 (accessed June 1, 2005).

da Bormida, G., and P. Lefrere. 2003. User presence in mobile environments. In *Being there: Concepts, effects and measurements of user presence in synthetic environments,* ed. G. Riva, F. Davide, and W. A. IJsselsteijn, 184–190. Amsterdam: Ios Press. http://www.vepsy.com/communication/book4/4_12BORMID.PDF (accessed June 1, 2005).

First International Digital, Inc. 2004. First International Digital and Mobile Internet Group (MIG) to provide mobile multimedia applications for China's largest wireless operator. April 6. http://www.fidinc.com/pr/pr_migchina.asp (accessed June 1, 2005).

InfoTrends/CAP Ventures. 2005. InfoTrends/CAP Ventures releases worldwide mobile imaging study results. January 11. http://www.infotrends-rgi.com/home/Press/itPress/2005/1.11.05.html (accessed June 1, 2005).

IT Facts. 2004. Mobile penetration in Taiwan and Hong Kong reaches 110% and 105.75%. Posting on IT Facts weblog, December 18. http://www.itfacts.biz/index.php?id=P2235 (accessed June 1, 2005).

J@pan Inc. 2001. Blowfish. April. http://www.japaninc.net/mag/comp/2001/04/apr01_blowfish.html (accessed June 1, 2005).

Kinzie, S. 2005. Colleges' land lines nearing silent end. *The Washington Post,* February 12. http://www.msnbc.msn.com/id/6955990 (accessed June 1, 2005).

McGuire, L., G. Roberts, and M. Moss. 2004. *Final report to QCA on the eVIVA project 2002–2004.* Chelmsford, Essex, UK: Ultralab Learning Technology Research Centre, Anglia Polytechnic University. http://slartibartfast.ultralab.net/%7Elesley/blog/archives/eviva_report.pdf (accessed June 1, 2005).

McNicol, T. 2004. Language e-learning on the move. *Japan Media Review,* April 5. http://ojr.org/japan/wireless/1080854640.php (accessed June 1, 2005).

Morita, M. 2003. The mobile-based learning (MBL) in Japan. Paper presented at the first Conference on Creating, Connecting and Collaborating through Computing, Kyoto, Japan, January. http://csdl.computer.org/comp/proceedings/c5/2003/1975/00/19750128.pdf (accessed June 1, 2005).

NOP World. 2005. Backpacks, lunch boxes and cells? . . . Nearly half of U.S. teens and tweens have cell phones, according to NOP World mKids study. March 9. http://www.nopworld.com/news.asp?go=news_item&key=151 (accessed June 1, 2005).

Norris, C., and E. Soloway. 2003. The viable alternative: handhelds. *The School Administrator* (Web edition), April. http://www.aasa.org/publications/sa/2003_04/soloway.htm (accessed June 1, 2005).

Papageorgiou, D., N. Ioannidis, I. Christou, M. Papathomas, and M. Diorinos. 2000. ARCHEOGUIDE: An augmented reality based system for personalized tours in cultural heritage sites. *Cultivate Interactive*, 1. http://www.cultivate-int.org/issue1/archeo/ (accessed June 1, 2005).

Raugust, K. 2004. Comicbook publishers dip their toes into digital delivery. *Animation World Magazine*, August 26. http://mag.awn.com/index.php?ltype=Special+Features&category2=Technology&article_no=2207 (accessed June 1, 2005).

Simon, E. 2004. U.S. wireless use behind rest of world. Associated Press, December 17. Posted to wireless network technologies forum on WirelessAdvisor.com. http://forums.wirelessadvisor.com/archive/index.php/t-6009.html (accessed June 1, 2005).

Stone, B. 2004. Your next computer. *Newsweek*, June 7. http://www.msnbc.msn.com/id/5092826/site/newsweek/ (accessed June 1, 2005).

Villafania, A. 2004. UP group turns mobile phone into learning platform. Infotech, INQ7.net. August 10. http://beta.inq7.net/infotech/index.php?index=1&story_id=3471 (accessed June 1, 2005).

Web Japan. 2004. Novels delivered to your phone. March 10. http://web-japan.org/trends/lifestyle/lif040310.html (accessed June 1, 2005).

23

The True 21st Century Literacy Is Programming

Power will soon belong to those who can master a variety of expressive human–machine interactions

Published in Edutopia *as*
"Programming is the New Literacy"

My goal is always to change people's thinking, so I was pleased when a former editor at Edutopia *told me that this essay had changed hers. I hope that some of these essays in this volume have changed some of your thinking as well. The importance of programming for our kids' future cannot be overstated. It is a particularly hard nut to crack in education, because we do not have enough K–12 teachers equipped to systematically teach it. But teach it we must, even if that means creating new tools and hiring new people. As Doug Rushkoff tells us in the title of his latest book, our young people's choice is to* Program or Be Programmed. *Fortunately a great many of our students are starting to program on their own (such as by creating their own apps), but this is not good enough. Programming, like problem solving, is a skill that should be infused into all our school subjects from math and science to social studies and English. Here's why.*

ଔ ଔ ଛ ଛ

Already, various thinkers about the future have proposed a number of candidates for the designation "21st century literacy." That is, what are the key skills humans must possess in order to be considered literate? Some writers assume that the definition of *literacy* will continue to be what it always has been: "The ability to carefully read and write a contemporary spoken language." Others specify that the term will apply only to fluency in one or more of the languages spoken by the largest numbers of people, those certain to be important over the next nine decades of the century; candidates include Spanish, English, or Mandarin Chinese.

Still others expand the notion of 21st century literacy beyond spoken and written language to include the panoply of skills often collected under the umbrella term *multimedia* (being able to both understand and create messages, communications, and works that include, or are constructed with, visual, aural, and haptic—that is, physical—elements as well as words). Some go on to find important emerging literacy in interactivity and games. And there are those who say it includes all of the above, and might include other factors as well.

I am one of these last, in that I believe fluency with multiple spoken languages will continue to be important, and that multimedia, interactivity, and other game-derived devices will be increasingly significant tools for communicating 21st century thought. Nonetheless, I firmly believe that the true key literacy of the new century lies outside all these domains.

I believe the single skill that will, above all others, distinguish a literate person is programming literacy, the ability to make digital technology do whatever, within the possible one wants it to do—to bend digital technology to one's needs, purposes, and will, just as in the present we bend words and images. Some call this skill human–machine interaction; some call it procedural literacy. Others just call it programming.

Seem strange? I'm sure it does. Today, people with highly developed skills in this area are seen as nerds. But consider that as machines become even more important components of our communication, our work, our education, our travel, our homes, and our leisure, the ability to make them do what we want will become increasingly valuable. Already, today, a former programmer in Seattle, one of these very nerds, is one of the richest people in the world.

So, in a sense, we are going to see as we progress through the 21st century a real revenge of the nerds, except that the new nerds will be our programmatically literate children. As programming becomes more important, it will leave the back room and become a key skill and attribute of our top intellectual and social classes, just as reading and writing did in the past. Remember, only a few centuries ago, reading and writing were confined to a small specialist class whose members we called scribes.

Do You HTML?

One might ask, "Will every educated person really have to program? Can't the people who need programming just buy it?" Possibly. Of course, with that model, we have in a sense returned to the Middle Ages or ancient Egypt, or even before. Then, if you needed to communicate your thoughts on paper, you couldn't do it yourself. You had to hire a better-educated person—a scribe—who knew the writing code. Then, at the other end, you needed someone to read or decode it—unless, of course, you were "well educated," that is, you had been taught to read and write and thus had become literate.

Classified Ad

Electronic Arts, the world's biggest video game company, recently created this billboard (see Figure 23.1) advertisement written in a programming language. Can you read it? (It says, "Now Hiring.")

Figure 23.1

Here's a key question: Will the need for a separate scribe tribe of programmers continue through the 21st century, or will the skill set of an educated person soon include programming fluency? I think that as programming becomes increasingly easy (which it will) and as the need to show rather than explain becomes important (which it will) and as people working together want to combine the results of their efforts and ideas instantaneously (which they will), educated people will, out of necessity, become programmers. Think of it: Your phone and car already require programming skills; many houses and jobs do, too. Programming will soon be how we interact with all our objects, and I believe it will be an important component of how we interact with one another as well.

Of course, there are already Luddites who think a digital machine is most elegant if it has only one button (like the Roomba robot floor cleaner) and people who keep searching for a cell phone that *only* makes phone calls. (Good luck.) There is a hierarchy of levels of making machines do what you want (that is, programming them) that runs from manipulating a single on-off switch to managing menus, options, and customization to coding higher-level programming languages (Flash, HTML, scripting) and lower-level languages (C++, Java) to creating assembler or machine language.

Few people, however, remain satisfied for long with the first level—as soon as we master that, most of us seek refinements and customization to our own needs and tastes. (The company that makes the Roomba offers a kit to turn its parts into whatever type of robot you want.)

Just about every young person programs (controls his or her own digital technology) to some extent. Many actions considered merely tasks—setting up a universal television remote, downloading a ringtone, customizing your mobile phone or desktop—are really programming. Doing a Web search is programming, as is using peer-to-peer or social-networking technologies, or eBay, or creating a document in Word, Excel, MySpace, or Facebook—and toss in building your avatar in Second Life. Today's kids are such good programmers that parents who buy expensive high-tech gadgets, such as camcorders or home theaters, often hand them to their children to set up (program) for them.

Today, most of this programming takes place in what I refer to as higher-level programming languages, consisting of menus and choices rather than the more flexible computer code. Of course, many people will be content with this level of programming (which still manages to baffle many "literate" adults).

But as today's kids grow up and become tomorrow's educated adults, most will go much further. At an early age, many young people learn the HTML language of Web pages and often branch out into its more powerful sister languages, such as XML and PHP. Other kids are learning programming languages like Game Maker, Flash, and Scratch, plus scripting language, graphics tools, and even C++, in order to build games. They learn them occasionally in school, but mostly on their own, after school, or in specialized summer camps. Why? First, because they realize it gives them the power to express themselves in the language of their own times, and second—and perhaps even more importantly—because they find it fun.

Want a Program? Hire a Kid

Suppose you have a need for a computer program. "Me?" you say. "Why would I have such a need?" But this possibility is not far-fetched at all. For instance, when Howard Dean ran for U.S. president a few years ago, he (or someone on his staff) had this idea: "What if we could collect contributions over the Internet?" Nobody had ever done this before, because the structure wasn't there—the program had never been written. So he went out and found a young programmer—an 18-year-old—to write the necessary code, and within only a matter of weeks the contributions started pouring in.

Most of us have problems a computer or another digital machine could easily solve for us, if only we conceived them as programming problems: "What is my best commuting route under different weather or other conditions?" "What are my statistics in my sports (or hobbies or work), and how do they compare with those of others?" "What is the optimal configuration of my [you name it]?" "How close am I to retirement, and will I have enough money?"

We all have ideas and needs amenable to programming solutions. My guess is that the more educated and literate we are (in the tired 20th century sense), the more of these we have. Yet most of us "Digital Immigrants"—those who came to computers and digital technology later in our lives—never even know it. We never realize that our desire to contact certain groups of people at certain times, or to lighten the load of repetitive work (say, grading papers), or to solve certain types of puzzles (like Sudoku), are really programming problems, and quite solvable ones at that.

But some among us do realize this, and we hire young people—often our kids, students, or employees but equally often consultants selling solutions—to do the necessary programming for us. One result is that we nonprogrammers often get ripped off (charged a lot for something quite simple), say, by financial planners offering seemingly sophisticated tools that, were we the slightest bit "literate," we could not only write ourselves but also customize specifically to our needs.

That's not how it will be in the future. As we move further into the 21st century, well-educated people who have needs and ideas addressable via programming will increasingly be able to recognize this fact and take matters into their own hands.

The Digital "Scribe Tribe"

Recently, programming languages "ordinary" people use have begun to emerge. Of these, one in particular—Flash, from Adobe—appears to be becoming a de facto standard. A great many kids in elementary school and the middle grades around the world are learning to program in Flash and are continually improving their skills as they advance through the grades. They use this tool and others like it (the Massachusetts Institute of Technology's Scratch, for example) to communicate a wide range of information and emotion—from stories to logic to games to ideas to persuasive arguments to works of art—all through programming. And it seems to them not nerdy but, rather, sophisticated and advanced.

The young people who do this vary greatly, of course, in the sophistication of what they can do. But sophisticated programming is becoming easier by the day. More and more premade programming objects—code written by others that can simply be plugged in to perform certain tasks—are available on the Internet, and are mostly free.

These databases of premade parts greatly enhance students' abilities, extend their programming and problem-solving capabilities, and shorten the time to get things done. In a sense, these bits of code are like an alphabet of programming. Recently, a friend was asked to program a "Wheel of Fortune" in Flash. Rather than taking a week to program it from scratch, he did a Web search, found something like what he wanted available free, and finished the project in an hour.

With these increasingly available and findable pieces of code, the range of what one can do and communicate with programming can expand indefinitely. And though simpler programs such as Flash already allow a pretty good degree of sophistication, many young people, through game creation, Internet-tool creation, or other means, get into the more sophisticated programming languages of three-dimensional world building, scripting, and entirely abstract, logical programming languages such as Java and C++.

And so emerges the new scribe tribe of programmers, reaching into (and eventually becoming) the intellectual elite of the 21st century. Programming has already become a tool today's young people use to communicate with one another via such components as machinima (see the definition below), ringtones, emoticons, searches, photo manipulation, and games. Young people email or IM (instant message) their creations to one another as we do our Word and Excel attachments, often posting them on the Internet for all to see. I bet few among us have not been the recent recipient of an emailed URL pointing us to an interesting program, a greeting card, a YouTube video, a machinima, or a game. (And, of course, Word and Excel are programming languages in themselves, with enormously sophisticated programming capabilities built in via macros and scripting.)

- Flash: A program that lets users create vector-based animation
- Machinima: "Machine cinema," in which simple tools found in video games are put to unexpected ends
- Scratch: An easy-to-use programming language developed by the Massachusetts Institute of Technology

As the century goes on, those who don't program—who can't bend their increasingly sophisticated computers, machines, cars, and homes to their wills and needs—will, I predict, be increasingly left behind. Parents and teachers often disrespect today's young people for being less than literate in the old reading-and-writing sense. But in turn, these young citizens of the future have no respect for adults who can't program a DVD player, a mobile phone, a computer, or anything else. Today's kids already see their parents and teachers as the illiterate ones. No wonder some teachers are scared to bring new technologies into the classroom—the kids just laugh at their illiteracy.

So, as the highly literate person of 2008 might [have started] off the day reading the *New York Times* and firing off a cleverly worded letter to the editor in response to a column, the highly literate person of 2028 may start the day ingesting the news in multiple ways with various types of stories they have programmed to be delivered in a preferred order, each at a preferred speed. And if that person feels a need to express an opinion, a simple bit of programming will allow him or her to determine all the people in the world to whom a response should go, and have it customized for each of them. Or one might program and fire off a video, an animation, or a simulation.

As the highly literate adult of today might pen a witty birthday card note for a young niece or nephew, the highly literate adult of tomorrow might program the child a game. And though today's highly literate person may enjoy a sophisticated novel or nonfiction book on a plane or train ride, tomorrow's highly literate person may prefer to change, by programming, whatever story or other media he or she is interacting with to suit individual preferences, and might then, with a little more programming, distribute those changes to the world.

And, of course, all this extends into the physical world as well thorough robotics and machine programming.

Tool Time

Tools have always been important to humans; now, intellectual tools are becoming increasingly significant. Until recently, getting an education and becoming a literate person meant learning to use the set of tools considered essential for each field or discipline. The tools in any endeavor change and improve over time, but they generally do so quite slowly, and new tools are often invented not by ordinary people but by "geniuses." Getting an education in a field has long meant gaining mastery of its existing tools.

In the 21st century, we will see, I think, something quite different. Using their ever more sophisticated programming skills, ordinary well-educated people will be constantly inventing new tools to solve whatever problems they have. In fact, this will be the expectation of what a literate person does. Already, in many circles (and not only scientific ones, although most are still rather geeky), one often hears someone say, "I wrote a little program to do that." And whether it's to find Manhattan addresses or to keep track of how many seconds remain until your next paycheck, a typical reaction is, "Can I get that?" to which the answer is as simple as a URL or a USB key.

It takes neither geeks nor armies of people to create useful tools via programming. A woman recently created an extremely useful program to compile and redeem her supermarket coupons. Google was created by two graduate students (Sergey Brin and Larry Page). Just one guy (Pierre Omidyar) developed the original program for eBay. Often, from these initial programming ideas come very big companies and profits. (Brin, Page, and Omidyar are all billionaires.)

But even if they don't yield huge profits, thousands—and soon millions—of people are beginning to create and share good programs we can all use free. Successful companies train new programmers, who then generate their own ideas and tools, in addition to the tools their companies build. Smart businesses are already searching for young people who can create these new tools—employees who are 21st century literate.

All of which brings us to an important question: If programming (the ability to control machines) is indeed the key literacy of this century, how do we, as educators, make our students literate? This problem is a particularly thorny one, because most teachers, even many of our best math and science instructors, do not possess the necessary skills, even rudimentary ones. Most of the tools (and even the concept of programming) were developed long after these teachers were born or schooled.

Can we do it by bringing working programmers into the schools? Not likely. Most of the good ones are busy programming and have no desire to teach.

The answer is not yet clear, but we can either come up with creative solutions to this real problem, or, in their absence, the kids will, as they are doing with so many things, figure out ways to teach themselves. Imagine: Literacy without (official) teachers.

Our machines are expected, thirty years from now, to be a billion times more powerful than they are today. Literacy will belong to those who can master not words, or even multimedia, but a variety of powerful, expressive human–machine interactions. If you are from the old school, you may not enjoy hearing this, but I doubt there is anything anyone can do to stop it.

Thirty years from now, will the United States be more competitive with a population that can read English at a tenth-grade level or with a population excellent at making the complex machines of that era do their bidding? The two options may be mutually exclusive, and the right choice may determine our children's place in the world's intellectual hierarchy.

Epilogue

From Digital Natives to Digital Wisdom

Homo Sapiens Digital

Published in Innovate

Initially there was some question on the part of my editor of whether to have this essay in this book, because it is less about education and schooling and more about the future of thinking and of humankind. But I wanted to include it because it points to a path that all educators will be trying to follow—and have their students follow—in the coming decades: the road toward "digital wisdom." While we are still in the process of defining what that is, I believe it is already clear that wisdom, in the digital age, means something quite different than it has in the past and demands new skills of all individuals. I am now in the process of turning these ideas into a book. I hope you will enjoy my explorations as I ponder some of these difficult and important issues in this final essay.

ଔ ଔ ଐ ଐ

The problems that exist in the world today cannot be
solved by the level of thinking that created them.

—Albert Einstein

In 2001, I published "Digital Natives, Digital Immigrants," a two-part article that explained these terms as a way of understanding the deep differences between the young people of today and many of their elders (Prensky 2001a, 2001b). Although many have found the terms useful, as we move further into the 21st century, into an age in which most people will be Digital Natives, the distinction between Digital Natives and Digital Immigrants is becoming less relevant. Clearly, we need to imagine a new set of distinctions helpful to those who are trying to help create and improve the future. I suggest we think in terms of digital wisdom.

Digital technology, I believe, can be used to make us not just smarter, but truly wiser. Digital wisdom is a two-fold concept, referring both to wisdom arising from the use of digital technology to access cognitive power beyond our usual capacity and to wisdom in the use of technology to enhance our innate capabilities. Because of technology, wisdom seekers, in the future, will have the previously unknown benefit of access to instant and ongoing world-wide discussions, all of recorded history, everything ever written, including massive libraries of case studies and data (ethical and otherwise) and years (or even centuries) of highly realistic, simulated experience. How, and how much, they make use of these resources, and how they filter through them (also with the aid of technology) will certainly have an important role in determining the wisdom of their decisions and judgments. Technology alone will not replace an intuitive sense of what's important, good judgment and problem-solving ability, and a clear moral compass. But, in an unimaginably complex future, the unenhanced person, however wise, will no longer be able to keep up with an enhanced human. That, I think, is the real reason to introduce technology into our educational system—in the future our young people won't have the necessary competitive wisdom without it.

Given that the brain is now generally accepted to be massively plastic, responding, changing, and adapting to the inputs it receives, it is even possible that the brains of people receiving all these inputs on a constant basis—i.e., searchers for wisdom—will be organized and structured differently in some ways from the brains of today's wise people. No one, of course, knows this for certain, but neuroscience is rapidly overturning previously accepted truths (such as the unchanging brain) at every turn. In the future, being considered "wise" may not be possible without the cognitive enhancements offered by increasingly sophisticated digital technology. Not that today's level of wisdom will not be possible—it may just not be desirable or sufficient in a technologically advanced world.

Digital Extensions and Enhancements

We are all moving, by fits and starts and each at our own speed, toward digital enhancement. In many ways, we are already there; digital enhancement is or will soon be available for just about everything we do. And this includes—here is the important part—cognition. Digital tools already extend and enhance our cognitive capabilities in a large variety of ways. Digital technology enhances memory, for example, via data input/output tools and electronic storage. Digital data-gathering and decision-making tools enhance judgment by allowing us to gather more data than we could on our own, helping us perform more complex analyses than we could unaided, and increasing our power to ask "what if?" and pursue all the implications of that question. Digital thought enhancement, provided by laptop computers, online databases, three-dimensional virtual simulations, online collaboration tools, PDAs, and a range of other, context-specific tools, is a reality in every profession, even in nontechnical fields such as law and the humanities.

We are already becoming dependent on these enhancements. As philosophers Andy Clark and David Chalmers (1998) argue, "extended cognition is a core cognitive process, not an add-on extra," as "the brain develops in a way that complements the external structures and learns to play its role within a unified, densely coupled system" ("3. Active Externalism," ¶17). As I recently heard a teenager say, expressing this idea more colloquially, "If I lose my cell phone, I lose half my brain." Many would express the same sentiment with regard to a PDA or a laptop computer; we are already embracing a basic level of digital enhancement, and we will accept ever more sophisticated enhancements as technology continues to develop.

These technologies, which will give us more direct access to their power by linking to our brains directly, are already here or on the horizon. Two recently released devices, one produced by Smart Brain Technologies and another by Emotive Systems, allow players to control the action in video games using their minds; NeuroSky is working on another version of the technology. The U.S. Air Force is experimenting with using similar technology to train pilots in hands-off flying (Satnews Daily 2008). Other emerging digital tools, such as voice stress analysis tools and automated translation utilities, facilitate communication and enhance understanding by revealing deception or providing more unbiased translations. As these tools become widely available, digital enhancement will become even more vital for everyone.

Digital Wisdom

What should we call this emerging digitally enhanced person? *Homo sapiens digital*, or wise digital human, perhaps. The key to understanding this development is to recognize that it includes *both* the digital and the wise. *Homo sapiens digital* differs from today's human in two key aspects: He or she accepts digital enhancement as an integral fact of human existence, and he or she is digitally wise, a trait exhibited both in the considered use of enhancements to complement his or her innate abilities and in the way and degree to which he or she uses enhancements to facilitate wiser decision making.

Wisdom, as any search will quickly show, is a universal, but ill-defined concept. Definitions of wisdom fill entire volumes. The *Oxford English Dictionary* suggests that wisdom's main component is judgment, referring to the "capacity judging rightly in matters relating to life and conduct, soundness of judgment in the choice of means and ends" (OED 1989). Philosopher Robert Nozick (1990) suggests that wisdom lies in knowing what's important; other definitions see wisdom as the ability to solve problems—what Aristotle called "practical wisdom" (Wikipedia 2009). Some definitions—although not all—attribute to wisdom a moral component, finding wisdom in the ability to discern the "right" or "healthy" thing to do. This is, of course, problematic, since agreement on moral issues is frequently difficult to come by. So wisdom cannot be conclusively defined without consideration of context as well. One interesting definition of wisdom, particularly useful in this discussion, comes from Howard Gardner (2000), who suggests that wisdom may be seen in the breadth of issues considered in arriving at a judgment or decision. Putting all these together, wisdom seems to refer to the ability to find practical, contextually appropriate, creative, and emotionally satisfying solutions to problems (as Solomon famously did with the baby problem). Many see it as a better, more complex version of mere problem solving.

As technology becomes increasingly more sophisticated, developing the capacity to help us make moral and ethical choices as well as more pragmatic decisions, what we call "human wisdom" will take on a new meaning. Some of that will come from the breadth of issues and resources the aspiring wise person can consider, as Gardner suggests. Another part will come from more, and deeper, experience, provided by hours of simulation, similar to what is required for today's airline pilots and astronauts. (The U.S. military is currently investigating ways to make its officers wiser faster in this way [source: private conversation].) It is also possible that reflection itself will be enhanced, as we are already seeing with the speed with which video game players review their previous games before they begin the next one. Future technological tools will allow people making judgments and decisions to review them in light of past experience, as today one can "backtest" a financial strategy on the historical market. And given the enhanced communications possibilities, wisdom will certainly involve a lot more sharing and testing of ideas while they are in formation.

Digital wisdom transcends the generational divide defined by the Immigrant/Native distinction. Many Digital Immigrants are digitally wise. Barack Obama, who grew up in the pre-digital era, showed his digital wisdom in enlisting the power of the Internet to enhance both his fundraising ability and his connection to the American people. Understanding that his judgment is enhanced by his ability to get instant feedback from his closest friends and advisors, he has refused to give up his BlackBerry. Rupert Murdoch, a self-confessed Digital Immigrant (Murdoch 2005), has also shown digital wisdom in recognizing the need to add digital news gathering and dissemination tools to his media empire.

The point is that while the need for wise people to discuss, define, compare, and evaluate perspectives isn't changing, the means that they use to do so, and the quality of their efforts, are growing more sophisticated because of digital technology. As a result, the unenhanced brain is well on its way to becoming insufficient for truly wise decision making. When we are all enhanced by implanted lie detectors, logic evaluators, executive function, and memory enhancements— all of which will likely arrive in our children's lifetimes—who among us will be considered wise? The advantage will go, almost certainly, to those who intelligently and prudently combine their innate capacities with their digital enhancements.

Wisdom Enhancement

So how can digital technology enhance our minds and lead to greater wisdom? One way to determine this is to ask where, as unenhanced humans, our mind now fails us, and explore how technology can enhance our capabilities in those arenas.

Unenhanced humans are limited in their perceptions and constrained by the processing power and functioning of the human brain. As a result, we tend to go astray in our thinking in ways that limit our wisdom:

- We make decisions based on only a portion of the available data.
- We make assumptions, often inaccurate, about the thoughts or intentions of others.
- We depend on educated guessing and verification (the traditional scientific method) to find new answers.
- We are limited in our ability to predict the future and construct what-if scenarios.
- We cannot deal well with complexity beyond a certain point.
- We cannot see, hear, touch, feel, or smell beyond the range of our senses.
- We find it difficult to hold multiple perspectives simultaneously.
- We have difficulty separating emotional responses from rational conclusions.
- We forget.

Some of these failures arise because we do not have access to necessary data, while others stem from our inability to conduct complex analyses, derive full understanding from the ever-increasing volumes of data available to us, understand others fully, or access alternative perspectives. They all reduce our innate capacity to judge, evaluate, and make practical decisions wisely. Fortunately, available and emerging digital tools can allow us to overcome these deficiencies and attain true digital wisdom.

Enhancing Our Access to Data

The human mind cannot remember everything; detailed, voluminous data is quickly lost. In some ways, this is good, in that it forces us to be selective, but it also limits our analytical capacity. Digital technology can help by providing databases and algorithms that gather and process vast amounts of data far more efficiently and thoroughly than the human brain can. Expert systems are one example of sophisticated digital tools that can help humans access a wider array of data. These systems gather the expertise of hundreds of human experts in one program to provide a more thorough assessment of a given situation than even a highly trained and experienced professional might be able to. One example of such a system is the Acute Physiology & Chronic Health Evaluation (APACHE) system, which helps doctors allocate scarce intensive-care resources to those patients most in need (see "Note: The APACHE System" below).

Few would consider it wise to use an expert system such as APACHE as the only decision maker; expert system technology is both imperfect and still in development. But would it be wise for a human to make the decisions without it? Wise decisions often involve not just ethical considerations, but also tradeoffs; in the context of a complex, delicate decision, like the one to remove a patient from intensive care, those tradeoffs can be difficult to assess. Expert systems and other sophisticated analytical tools allow for a fuller understanding of the risks and benefits inherent in a decision.

Enhancing Our Ability to Conduct Deeper Analyses

In an article provocatively titled "The End of Theory," writer Chris Anderson (2008) describes how the massive amounts of data now being collected and stored by Google and others are allowing a new type of scientific analysis. In many cases, scientists no longer have to make educated guesses, construct hypotheses and models, and test them with data-based experiments and examples. Instead, they can mine the complete set of data for patterns that reveal effects, producing scientific conclusions *without* the need to experiment further, because they rely on analysis of a complete, digitally stored data set. In a similar way, Google's advertising tools draw valid and useful conclusions about what works in advertising without actually knowing anything either about what is advertised or about the consumers of the advertising. The software does these things based purely on sophisticated analyses of available data; the analyses improve as the amount of data increases (as it does exponentially), and the analysis tools improve as well. This is the same principle, according to Anderson, that allows Google to "translate languages without actually 'knowing' them (given equal corpus data, Google can translate Klingon into Farsi as easily as it can translate French into German)" (2008, ¶5). Here, too, the tools will improve as more data becomes available. Imagine what will happen when the entire universe of everything ever written is available for analysis.

This approach reverses the generally accepted nature of the human/machine coupling—rather than the mind imagining possibilities that the data confirms or denies, the data announce facts and relationships and the human either looks for explanations, or—as Google does with advertising—uses the relationships to achieve success without knowing or caring why they exist. Surely, such ability should lead us to question what wisdom is in such situations, and the relationship between mind and machine in producing wisdom in a digital future. Future wisdom will involve as much finesse in eliciting relationships as in imagining them.

On the other hand, there are areas where a human mind's ability to interpret and evaluate data will be crucial to attaining digital wisdom. From warfare to architecture to politics, asking "what if?" has always been critical to understanding complex systems, and human wisdom has always included the ability to what-if well. While simulation, practiced for thousands of years in sandbox, mechanical, and thought experiments, is a sophisticated way to explore possible interpretations of data, unenhanced humans are limited in the number of options, intermediate states, and end states that they can explore in this way. Pairing human intelligence with digital simulation allows the mind to progress further and faster. The human ability to interpret and evaluate the models underlying the simulations plays a large role in using them wisely. In the future, more sophisticated simulation algorithms will allow humans to exercise their imaginative capacity in ever-more complex what-if constructions, allowing for more thorough exploration of possibilities and wiser decisions. With the introduction of modern simulation games such as Sim City, Roller Coaster Tycoon, and Spore, this kind of digital wisdom enhancement already begins at a very early age.

Enhancing Our Ability to Plan and Prioritize

As the world becomes more complex, planning and prioritization far beyond the capability of the unenhanced human brain will be required; digital enhancements will be needed to help us to anticipate second- and third-order effects that the unaided mind may be blind to. The full implications of massive undertakings like human space travel, the construction of artificial cities in the Arabian Sea, the building of huge machines such as large hadron colliders, and complex financial dealings (such as those that have recently wrought havoc on the economy) cannot be competently perceived and assessed by even the wisest unaided minds. Alan Greenspan, for example, is widely considered one of our wisest financial gurus; and yet, his assessment of the fundamental workings of our economy was mistaken: "You know," he admitted in a congressional hearing in October 2008, "that's precisely the reason I was shocked, because I have been going more than 40 years or more with very considerable evidence that it was working considerably well" (Leonhardt 2008). Humans will require digital enhancement in order to achieve a full understanding of these increasingly complex issues—and a full sense of the practical wisdom of pursuing them. We currently do not have, in many areas, either the databases of past successes and failures, or the tools to analyze them, that are required to enhance our wisdom and collective memory—but we will going forward.

Enhancing Our Insight Into Others

One of the greatest barriers to human understanding and communication is that we cannot see inside another person's mind. This limitation gives rise to unintended misunderstandings and allows people to employ all sorts of deceptive strategies, both consciously and unconsciously. Some of the ways digital technology is helping us overcome this barrier include various means of truth (or lie) detection, multimodal communications, and digital readouts of our own and others' brain waves. Already, researchers at Carnegie-Mellon University (CMU), using digital computer analysis of brain patterns captured by fMRI scans, are able to tell what a person is thinking about (Mitchell et al. 2008). It is likely, according to these researchers, that our children will see in their lifetimes the ability to read people's thoughts, and even direct brain-to-brain communication. While this will clearly raise ethical issues and privacy questions that will have to be addressed, there can be little doubt that as people gain access to and learn to take into account others' unspoken motives, thoughts, needs, and judgments in their own thinking, their wisdom will increase.

Enhancing Our Access to Alternative Perspectives

The world is full of things we cannot perceive unenhanced, things that are too small, too large, too fast, too abstract, too dangerous, or outside the range of our unaided senses. Exploring these things through digital enhancements will certainly help expand both our understanding of these things and our knowledge about how they can help or hurt us. It will also expand our ability to assume multiple perspectives—to see things from more than one point of view—and, hence, our wisdom. Perception of things outside our normal range can be enhanced digitally in numerous ways, from manipulable three-dimensional simulations to digitally monitored biofeedback to control of our mental and sensory states, which may also enhance memory and emotional control. Alternative perspectives can also be gained through increasingly sophisticated digital role playing, using simulations which take people through large numbers of difficult and critical situations from partisan and observers' points of view.

There are, undoubtedly, other ways in which digital technology will, in our own or our children's lives, enhance our understanding and wisdom. None of these tools will replace the human mind; rather, they will enhance our quest for knowledge and our development of wisdom.

Objections to Digital Enhancement

Not everyone accepts the power of digital enhancement to make us both smarter and wiser. On its July/August 2008 cover, *The Atlantic* magazine asks "Is Google Making Us Stupid?" Google is a stand-in for the Internet and digital technology more generally. The author's concern is that digital enhancements such as the Internet make our natural minds lazier and less able (Carr 2008). While that is certainly something we should guard against, we must also bear in mind that new technologies have always raised similar objections; as Carr points out, in Plato's *Phaedrus,* Socrates objects to writing on the basis that it undermines the memory.

In fact, what's happening now is very much the opposite: digital technology is making us smarter. Steven Johnson has documented this in *Everything Bad Is Good for You* (2005), in which he argues that the new technologies associated with contemporary popular culture, from video games to the Internet to television and film, make far more cognitive demands on us than did past forms, increasing our capabilities in a wide variety of cognitive tasks. As Johnson puts it, "Today's popular culture may not be showing us the righteous path. But it is making us smarter" (14). Socrates was correct in his fear that writing would diminish our memories, but shortsighted in that concern. While we may remember less and memorize less readily than did humans in Socrates's day, the addition of writing has made us considerably wiser by expanding our collective memory as well as our ability to share information across time and distance.

Worries that ubiquitous GPS systems might diminish our map-reading ability or that spell checkers and calculators will result in a generation that cannot spell or do mental math are similarly short-sighted. Every enhancement comes with a tradeoff: we gave up huge mental memory banks when we started writing things down; we gave up the ability to tell time by the sun when we began carrying pocket watches. But we gained a set of shared cultural memories and a more precise notion of time that fueled the industrial revolution. Digital wisdom arises from the combination of the mind and digital tools; what the unenhanced mind loses by outsourcing mundane tasks will be more than made up for by the wisdom gained. Wisdom, particularly practical wisdom, must be understood in light of the digital enhancements that make it stronger.

Being Digitally Wise

So what makes a digitally wise person? What habits do the digitally wise use to advance their capabilities in this area and the capabilities of those around them for whom they may have authority or responsibility? Can digital wisdom be taught?

Examples of digital wisdom are all around us. Leaders are digitally wise when they use available techniques to connect with their constituents for polling, contributions, and participation, as Barack Obama did so well in the 2008 U.S. presidential campaign. Journalists are digitally wise when they take advantage of participative technologies such as blogs and wikis to enlarge their perspectives and those of their audience. Nicolas Carr, for example, the author of the Google article referenced above, posted his notes and sources in his blog in response to reader requests for more information (available at http://www.roughtype.com/archives/2008/08/is_google_makin.php).

Digital wisdom can be, and must be, learned and taught. As we offer more courses in digital literacy, we should also offer students guidance in developing digital wisdom. Parents and educators are digitally wise when they recognize this and prepare the children in their care for the future. Educators are digitally wise when they let students learn by using new technologies, putting themselves in the role of guides, context providers, and quality controllers. And parents are digitally wise when, recognizing the extent to which the future will be mediated by technology, they encourage their children to use digital technology wisely.

The digitally wise distinguish between digital wisdom, mere digital literacy, and digital cleverness, and they do their best to eradicate digital dumbness when it arises. They know that just knowing how to use particular technologies makes one no wiser than just knowing how to read words. Digital wisdom means not just manipulating technology easily, or even creatively; it means making wiser decisions because one is enhanced by technology. Therefore, the digitally wise look for the cases where technology enhances thinking and understanding. No digitally wise leader would make any major decision, no digitally wise scientist would come to any conclusion, without digital tools enhancing their own thinking. They may rely on intuition, but that intuition is informed, inspired, and supported by digital enhancements and by the additional data digital tools provide. Those who are truly digitally wise do not resist their digitally enhanced selves, but accept them gladly.

Being digitally wise involves not only enhancing our natural capabilities with existing technologies, but also continuously identifying additional areas where our natural human tools—even when they are developed to a very high level—cannot do the job unaided. As new digital tools appear, especially ones that take hold in a strong way, the digitally wise seek them out actively. They investigate and evaluate the positives as well as the negatives of new tools and figure out how to strike the balance that turns tools into wisdom enhancers. The digitally wise also realize that the ability to control digital technology, to bend it to their needs, is a key skill in the digital age. So they are interested in programming, in the broadest sense of making machines do what people want them to.

Conclusion

In the lifetimes of our children, much more powerful digital mental enhancements—the embedded chips and brain manipulations of science fiction—will become a reality, just as gene manipulation, long considered a far-off dream, is with us now. Just as we have begun to confront the ethical, moral, and scientific challenges presented by genetic medicine, we will have to confront the issue of digital wisdom sooner or later, and we will be better off doing it sooner. Many of these enhancements will bring ethical dilemmas, but the digitally wise will distinguish between true ethical issues (Is the enhancement safe? Is it available equally to all?) and mere preferences and prejudices.

Nobody suggests that people should stop using and improving their unaided minds. But I am opposed to those who claim the unenhanced mind and unaided thinking are somehow superior to the enhanced mind. To claim this is to deny all of human progress, from the advent of writing to the printing press to the Internet. Thinking and wisdom have become, in our age, a symbiosis of the human brain and its digital enhancements.

I do not think technology is wise in itself (although some day it may be) or that human thinking is no longer necessary or important. It is from the interaction of the human mind and digital technology that the digitally wise person is coming to be. I believe it is time for the emerging digitally wise among us, youth and adults alike, to refuse to be intimidated by the unenhanced. With our eyes wide open to enhancement's potential harm as well as its benefits, let us bring our colleagues, students, teachers, parents, and peers to the digital wisdom of the 21st century.

Note: The APACHE System

The Acute Physiology & Chronic Health Evaluation (APACHE) system was created by medical researchers and doctors seeking a better way to determine, when beds became scarce, which patients should be retained in a hospital's intensive care unit. The system worked by comparing key statistics for a particular patient with millions of cases with similar characteristics to project likely outcomes. The system capsulized its analysis into a number for each patient, the APACHE score. A higher score meant that the patient stayed in intensive care; a lower score meant the patient left.

It seems startling that a single, computer-generated number could even be considered useful in making such a potentially life-and-death decision, even more so that it could carry as much weight as a doctor's personal evaluation. The reasoning behind this is that there are some things the human brain is very good at, but by nature it tends to over-focus on two things: the recent and the unusual. While that sometimes serves us very well, it is much better, for a decision like this, to take into account every relevant case. That is something that, in an unaided state, the human mind is just not capable of doing.

The point is not that machines are better than the human mind. The point is that the mind and the machine together produce the wisest decisions. As one study puts it "[APACHE III] has been shown to be predictive of in-hospital mortality rate. It has performed equally well in community based and academic settings. [But] the APACHE, like other scoring systems presents some limitations. It is dependent on an operator and requires a long period of training to be used efficiently."[P. Murabito, F. Ribulotta, and A. Gullo, "Quality Management in the ICU: Understanding the Process and Improving the Art." In *Anaesthesia Pain, Intensive Care and Emergency Medicine*, A. Gullo, ed. Proceedings of the 22nd post graduate course in critical care medicine, Venice-Mestre Italy, November 9–11, 2007 (Springer, 2008), Chapter 33, p. 349.]

References

Anderson, C. 2008. The end of theory: The data deluge makes the scientific method obsolete. *Wired Magazine* 16 (7). http://www.wired.com/science/discoveries/magazine/16–07/pb_theory (accessed January 28, 2009). Archived at http://www.webcitation.org/5eBIPrc60.

Carr, N. 2008. Is Google making us stupid?: What the Internet is doing to our brains. *The Atlantic* 301 (6): 56–63. http://www.theatlantic.com/doc/200807/google (accessed January 28, 2009). Archived at http://www.webcitation.org/5eBJxMMM3.

Clark, A., and D. J. Chalmers. 1998. The extended mind. *Analysis* 58: 7–19. http://consc.net/papers/extended.html (accessed January 28, 2009). Archived at http://www.webcitation.org/5eBEF2Ncm.

Gardner, H. 2000. *Intelligence reframed: Multiple intelligences for the 21st century.* New York: Basic Books.

Johnson, S. B. 2005. *Everything bad is good for you.* New York: Riverhead Books.

Leonhardt, D. 2008. Greenspan's mea culpa. [Weblog entry, October 23.] *Economix.* http://economix.blogs.nytimes.com/2008/10/23/greenspans-mea-culpa/ (accessed January 28, 2009). Archived at http://www.webcitation.org/5eBJTVMJi.

Mitchell, T., S. V. Shinkareva, A. Carlson, K. Chang, V. L. Malave, R. A. Mason, and M. A. Just. 2008. Predicting human brain activity associated with the meanings of nouns. *Science* 320 (May): 1191–1195.

Murdoch, R. 2005. Speech to the American Society of Newspaper Editors, April 13. http://www.newscorp.com/news/news_247.html (accessed January 26, 2009). Archived at http://www.webcitation.org/5e6jPyqgB.

Nozick, R. 1990. *The examined life: Philosophical meditations.* New York: Simon & Schuster-Touchstone, 1990.

OED. 1989. "Wisdom," definition 1a. *Oxford English Dictionary*, 2nd. ed. Oxford: Oxford University Press.

Prensky, M. 2001a. Digital natives, digital immigrants. *On the Horizon* 9 (5): 1–6. http://www.scribd.com/doc/9799/Prensky-Digital-Natives-Digital-Immigrants-Part1 (accessed January 28, 2009). Archived at http://www.webcitation.org/5eBDYI5Uw.

Prensky, M. 2001b. Digital natives, digital immigrants, part 2: Do they really think differently? *On the Horizon* 9 (6): 1–6. http://www.twitchspeed .com/site/Prensky%20-%20Digital%20Natives,%20Digital%20 Immigrants%20-%20Part2.htm (accessed January 28, 2009). Archived at http://www.webcitation.org/5eBDhJB2N.

Satnews Daily. 2008. Hands off F-16 lands using Lockheed Martin computer control technology. *Satnews Daily,* December 11. http://www.satnews .com/cgi-bin/story.cgi?number=1057554591 (accessed January 28, 2009). Archived at http://www.webcitation.org/5eBFSBrSt.

Wikipedia. 2009. Wisdom. http://en.wikipedia.org/wiki/Wisdom (accessed January 26, 2009). Archived at http://www.webcitation.org/5e6jXGyZN.

QUESTIONS FOR REFLECTION

1. How can we best define the role of technology in learning and the classroom? Why is it important for us to do this?

2. How much "backup education" do we need to provide to our 21st century students?

3. What simple things can all teachers do that will have a huge impact on their teaching effectiveness?

4. Why is video so important to our students' education and future? How should educators be using it?

5. Can computer games be used to teach important school lessons? How? Why would we do this?

6. Why is "mutual respect" so important to learning?

7. What can teachers do to help eliminate the so-called digital divide?

8. What is the difference between "search" and "research"? Why does it matter?

9. What role should computer simulation play in 21st century teaching and learning?

10. How can cell phones be used to improve teaching and students' learning?

11. Why is programming important for our students' future? How can we best teach it?

12. What is "digital wisdom"? Can we reach it? Why does this matter?

Final Note

You can read my further thoughts on the topics discussed here (and on many other topics) on my website, www.marcprensky .com, and in my forthcoming books:

Brain Gain: Technology and the Quest for Digital Wisdom from Palgrave Macmillan

and

Problem-Solving, Passion, and Producing the Right Stuff (tentative title) from Corwin.

Best,
Marc Prensky

Credits

Part 1. Rethinking Education

1. The Reformers Are Leaving Our Schools in the 20th Century
Originally published January 24, 2011, in *SNS Newsletter.* Copyright by Marc Prensky.

2. On Learning
Originally published in 2003 in *On the Horizon, 11*(1), 26–32. Copyright by Marc Prensky.

3. Education as Rocket Science
Originally published in 2009 in *Educational Technology Magazine, 49*(6), 64, where Marc's column, "New Issues, New Answers," appears regularly. Copyright by Marc Prensky.

4. Turning On the Lights
Originally published March 2008 in *Educational Leadership, 65*(6), 40–45. Copyright by Marc Prensky.

5. Digital Natives, Digital Immigrants
Part I:
Originally published in 2001 in *On the Horizon, 9*(5), 1–6. Copyright by Emerald Group Publishing. Reproduced with permission.
Part II:
Originally published in 2001 in *On the Horizon, 9*(6), 1–6. Copyright by Emerald Group Publishing. Reproduced with permission.

6. The Emerging Online Life of the Digital Native
Copyright 2004 by Marc Prensky.

7. Young Minds, Fast Times
Originally published May 30, 2010, in *Edutopia.* Copyright by Edutopia .org; The George Lucas Foundation.

8. Blame Our Young? Or Use Their Passion!
Copyright 2010 by Marc Prensky.

9. To Educate, We Must Listen
Copyright 2007 by Marc Prensky.

10. Bringing the Future to School: The Prensky Challenge
Copyright 2006 by Marc Prensky.

11. Open Letter to the Bill & Melinda Gates Foundation
Copyright 2006 by Marc Prensky.

Part 2. 21st Century Learning, and Technology in the Classroom

12. The Role of Technology in Teaching and the Classroom
Originally published Nov-Dec 2008 in *Educational Technology Magazine,* where Marc's column, "New Issues, New Answers," appears regularly. Copyright by Marc Prensky.

13. Backup Education?
Originally published in Jan-Feb 2008 in *Educational Technology Magazine, 48*(1), where Marc's column, "New Issues, New Answers," appears regularly. Copyright by Marc Prensky.

14. Simple Changes in Current Practices May Save Our Schools
Originally published July 12, 2010, in *ETC Online Journal.* Licensed under a Creative Commons Attribution 3.0 Unported License.

15. The Longer View: Why YouTube Matters
Originally published in 2010 in *On the Horizon, 18*(2). Copyright by Emerald Group Publishing. Reproduced with permission.

16. Beyond the Lemonade Stand
Originally published in *Don't Bother Me Mom—I'm Learning,* by M. Prensky, 2006, St. Paul, MN: Paragon House. Copyright by Paragon House. Reproduced with permission.

17. Types of Learning and Possible Game Styles
Originally published in *Digital Game-Based Learning,* by M. Prensky, 2007, St. Paul, MN: Paragon House. Copyright by Paragon House. Reproduced with permission.

18. On Being Disrespected
Originally published October 2006 in *Educational Leadership, 64*(2). Copyright by Marc Prensky.

19. Let's Be "Digital Multipliers"
Originally published Jan-Feb 2009 in *Educational Technology Magazine,* where Marc's column, "New Issues, New Answers," appears regularly. Copyright by Marc Prensky.

20. Search Versus Research
Copyright 2005 by Marc Prensky.

21. Simulation Nation
Originally published August 1, 2007, in *Edutopia.* Copyright by Edutopia .org; The George Lucas Foundation.

22. What Can You Learn From a Cell Phone? Almost Anything!
This article was originally published in *Innovate* (http://www.innovate online.info/) as: Prensky, M. 2005. What can you learn from a cell phone? Almost anything!. *Innovate* 1(5). http://www.innovateonline.info/index .php?view=article&id=83 (accessed April 24, 2008). The article is reprinted here with permission of the publisher, The Fischler School of Education and Human Services at Nova Southeastern University.

23. The True 21st Century Literacy Is Programming
Originally published January 13, 2008, in *Edutopia.* Copyright by Edutopia.org; The George Lucas Foundation.

Epilogue: From Digital Natives to Digital Wisdom
This article was originally published in *Innovate* (http://www.innovate online.info/) as: Prensky, M. 2009. H. sapiens digital: From digital immigrants and digital natives to digital wisdom. *Innovate* 5(3). http://www.innovateon line.info/index.php?view=article&id=705 (accessed February 4, 2009). The article is reprinted here with permission of the publisher, The Fischler School of Education and Human Services at Nova Southeastern University.

Index

CORWIN
A SAGE Company

The Corwin logo—a raven striding across an open book—represents the union of courage and learning. Corwin is committed to improving education for all learners by publishing books and other professional development resources for those serving the field of PreK–12 education. By providing practical, hands-on materials, Corwin continues to carry out the promise of its motto: **"Helping Educators Do Their Work Better."**